# WINGS OF THE MORNING

If I ascend up into heaven, thou art there…
If I take the wings of the morning,
and dwell in the uttermost parts of the sea;
Even there shall thy hand lead me…

*Psalm 139*

# WINGS OF THE MORNING

## The life of Captain James Belgrave

Dennis Edensor

DIAMOND D PUBLISHING
2006

The cover illustration Surprise Attack, by Barry Weekley, depicts James Belgrave
in action flying his SE5a while with No 60 Squadron in the summer of 1918

ISBN 0-9548400-0-3


First published in Great Britain 2006 by

DIAMOND D PUBLISHING
16 Avon Fields
Welford, Northampton NN6 6JL

Printed in England by Warwick Printing Company Limited, Leamington Spa

# CONTENTS

# ACKNOWLEDGEMENTS

Many people gave generously of their time and knowledge to help bring this modest book to fruition. In particular, Robert R D Belgrave cheerfully endured a stranger's probings into his family's history and provided wonderful photographs. The late Michael De-la-Noy gave permission for the use of facts from his eminently readable history of Bedford School, while Stuart and Beryl Blythe also helped with the Bedford connection. Wing Commander C G 'Jeff' Jefford, author of *The Flying Camels*, the definitive history of No 45 Squadron, provided valuable pointers. Photographs were supplied by James A Brown, G Stuart Leslie and Squadron Leader D W 'Joe' Warne. Dr Gill Cookson and Dr Liz O'Donnell allowed me to plunder the results of their researches into the history of Quakers in the North East. The enthusiastic response of Dino Lemonofides, of the Oxfordshire and Buckinghamshire Light Infantry Museum, to queries about the regiment was particularly helpful. In Switzerland, Evelyne Lüthi-Graf, of the Archives de Montreux, and the Reverend Andrew Ling, of St John's, Territet, provided a warm welcome as well as much useful information.

Major John Mansel supplied details about his family's connection to the Belgraves and Pat Whelehan took the author on a tour of Belgrave-related locations in Chinnor. The guidance of First World War aviation experts Norman Franks and Graham Berry proved invaluable and Peter Steinkamp delved into the German records. The staff of the National Archives, Imperial War Museum, National Army Museum, National Maritime Museum and RAF Museum were unfailingly ready with guidance, as were the staff of Darlington Library and the local records offices of Leicestershire, Buckinghamshire and Oxfordshire. Miles Hedley read the draft for errors and made helpful suggestions, Barry Crowther helped prepare the photographs for reproduction and Andrew Sanderson provided technical assistance. Steve Mayer designed the cover while the maps are the painstaking work of Clive Bradley. Many years ago, when Great War records were less accessible, it was Humphrey Wynn, then of the Air Historical Branch, Ministry of Defence, who showed the way. Thanks to them all.

# THE ILLUSTRATIONS

(i) The ribbon of the Military Cross worn by James Belgrave in this formal photograph proves the picture was taken after June 1917. *(Robert R D Belgrave)*

(ii) Charles Dalrymple Belgrave, James's brother, aged 18. On the rear of the original photograph are the handwritten words *Charles Dalrymple Belgrave taken September 1913 by James Dacres Belgrave.* Charles was a keen photographer and it seems reasonable to surmise that he set up the camera and posed, asking his younger brother to 'press the button'. *(Author's collection)*

(iii) The Reverend Charles Belgrave, James's great-uncle and the last Belgrave to be Rector of North Kilworth. *(From a 1901 memorial card)*

(iv) Eustace Mansel, James's uncle, as a young man before his military career. *(Major John Mansel)*

(v) Dalrymple James Belgrave, barrister father of James. The arms of the Belgrave family are in the centre of the page. *(Robert R D Belgrave)*

(vi) The chalet in the early 20th Century picture of the Belgrave brothers at Les Avants still stands and the narcissi continue to flourish. It has not been possible to confirm that the woman in the photograph is the boys' mother Isabella. *(Robert R D Belgrave)*

(vii) Villa Victoria at Clarens in the late 19th Century. *(via Archives de Montreux)*

(viii) Belgrave's birthplace in Pitt Street, Kensington, as it is today. *(Author)*

(ix) Merton Road, Bedford, home to James Belgrave as a schoolboy. *(Author)*

(x) County End. The Belgraves' former home in Chinnor has been much updated since this photograph was taken in the 1980s. *(Author)*

(xi) Unfortunately the names of James Belgrave's classmates in the picture taken at Bedford Grammar School a year or two before the Great War are not known. One wonders how many of those young men served in the conflict and how many survived. *(Robert R D Belgrave)*

(xii) It is known that the picture of James and Charles Belgrave with their friend was taken in 1915 because James is not wearing RFC wings on his tunic. The chum, whose name is given as Hayman, looks like the boy, second left on the rear row of the previous picture. Certainly the brothers had a schoolmate called Hayman. *(Robert R D Belgrave)*

(xiii) The photograph of James Belgrave at Le Touquet is undated. His blazer bears the badge of Bedford School's second rowing VIII. *(Robert R D Belgrave)*

(xiv) Dalrymple Belgrave in the uniform of the Bucks Volunteers in late 1916 when he was aged 65. *(Robert R D Belgrave)*

(xv) James Belgrave's first combat report, handwritten after he tangled with an enemy aircraft on Christmas Eve 1916. *(By courtesy of the National Archives, formerly Public Record Office, reference AIR 1/1786/204/151/1)*

(xvi) Belgrave (second from right) holds one of No 45 Squadron's unofficial pet dogs in 1917. With him are 2nd Lt J A Vessey (third from left), Lt H E R Fitchat (fourth from left) and 2nd Lt F H Austin (extreme right). *(This is one of a marvellous collection of No 45 Squadron photographs held by James A Brown whose father was a boyhood friend of Captain M B Frew, the squadron's most successful pilot of the First World War)*

(xvii) Belgrave (far right) with No 45 Squadron observers (from left) 2nd Lt Austin, 2nd Lt F G Truscott and unknown. *(James A Brown)*

(xviii) Sopwith 1½-Strutter A1114 was used by No 28 Training Squadron so it is possible that Belgrave flew this machine. He also flew several examples of the type while with No 45 Squadron *(G Stuart Leslie)*

(ixx) Belgrave at Ste-Marie-Cappel in 1917. *(James A Brown)*

(xx) James Belgrave in trench coat while on home defence duties at Rochford with (from left) Lt P Thompson, Lt L F Hutcheon and Lt J E C Macvicker. *(James A Brown)*

(xxi) Sopwith Pup A653 was the actual machine in which Belgrave survived a low-level collision with an Avro 504 while serving with No 61 (HD) Squadron. *(G Stuart Leslie)*

(xxii) This SE5a is the type of aircraft flown by Belgrave at No 61 (HD) Squadron and later with No 60 Squadron. The picture is of Captain H C Stroud, who flew with Belgrave at No 61. The machine is probably B679, which Stroud was flying when he was killed in a mid-air collision over Essex. *(G Stuart Leslie)*

(xxiii) The brass memorial plaque to James Belgrave in the chancel of St Andrew's church, North Kilworth. *(Author)*

(xxiv) James Belgrave's headstone in Grove Town Cemetery, near Albert, Somme. *(Author)*

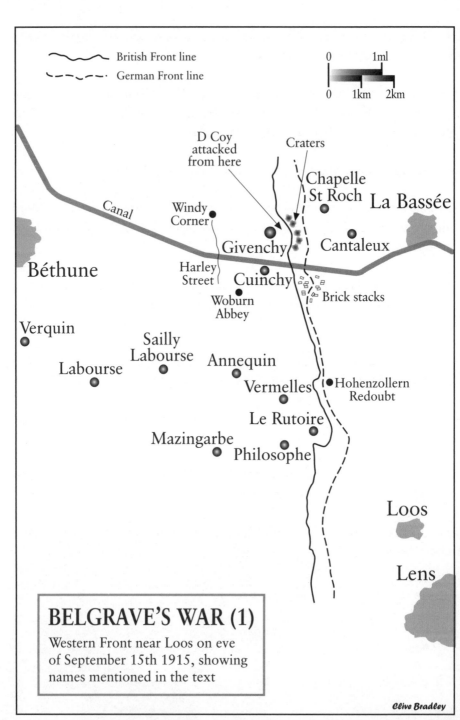

British Front line

German Front line

0 1ml

0 1km 2km

D Coy attacked from here

Craters

Canal

Windy Corner

Chapelle St Roch

La Bassée

Givenchy

Cantaleux

Béthune

Harley Street

Cuinchy

Woburn Abbey

Brick stacks

Verquin

Sailly Labourse

Labourse

Annequin

Vermelles

Hohenzollern Redoubt

Le Rutoire

Mazingarbe

Philosophe

Loos

Lens

## BELGRAVE'S WAR (1)

Western Front near Loos on eve of September 15th 1915, showing names mentioned in the text

Clive Bradley

Dunkirk

Roulers

Poperinghe ● Passchendaele
● Ypres ● Zonnebeke
Cassell ● Abeele ● Vlamertinge ● Becelaere
Clairmarais ○ Dickebusch ● Menin
Ste-Marie-Cappel ○ Lake ● Comines
St Omer ○ Bailleul ○
Ploegsteert ●
Armentières ●

Lille

● Béthune

**BELGRAVE'S WAR (2)**

‑ ‑ ‑ ‑ ‑ ‑ Front line in
early 1917 when Belgrave
was with 45 Sqdn

● Places named in text
○ RFC aerodromes

● Lens ● Douai

Arras ●

Cambrai ●

0   5mls   10mls

0   5km   10km   15km

● Bapaume

*Clive Bradley*

xiii

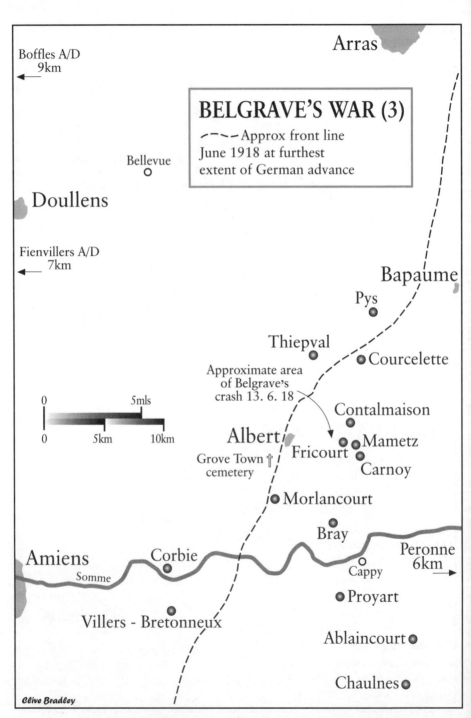

Boffles A/D
9km
←

Bellevue
○

Doullens

Fienvillers A/D
7km
←

**BELGRAVE'S WAR (3)**

‑ ‑ ‑ Approx front line
June 1918 at furthest
extent of German advance

Arras

Bapaume

Pys
●

Thiepval
●

Courcelette ●

Approximate area
of Belgrave's
crash 13. 6. 18

Contalmaison
●

0        5mls
⌶━━━━━━⌶━━━━━━⌶
0        5km      10km

Albert

Fricourt ● Mametz
Carnoy

Grove Town †
cemetery

Morlancourt ●

Bray
●

Amiens                   Corbie
Somme              ●

Peronne
6km
→

Cappy
○

Proyart
●

Villers - Bretonneux
●

Ablaincourt ●

Chaulnes ●

*Clive Bradley*

xiv

# INTRODUCTION

# DESTINY AT DAWN

FOUR British biplanes bounced free of the furrowed grass and climbed into a sombre Somme dawn. At the controls of the leading, single-seat scout aircraft was Captain James Belgrave who, satisfied that his comrades were tucking into position, headed east towards the lines. The fliers' task that dull June morning in 1918 was to carry out an offensive patrol, taking the war to the enemy's own airmen for as long as reserves of fuel, ammunition, daring and luck permitted. Belgrave, a seasoned veteran of the air conflict, was well qualified to command such a mission. The newly awarded bar to his Military Cross testified to the courage and prowess as a pilot which had earned him seventeen victories in the skies above the Western Front. His leadership qualities were such that he had the respect of senior officers and the loyalty of his pilots and ground crew in equal measure.

Huddled in his cockpit against the chill blast of the slipstream, Belgrave understood fully the importance of his role. To succeed in sending one or perhaps two German machines crashing to earth may have seemed an insignificant contribution in a war where a day's infantry casualties could number hundreds, even thousands. However, both sides had learnt long since the value of aircraft in directing artillery fire or monitoring and harrying the enemy's ground troops. The shooting-down of the foe's observer machines or the deadly, darting scouts protecting them was work as vital as it was perilous and nerve-shredding.

Within half an hour of take-off from its squadron's makeshift aerodrome the patrol was over the lines at 9,000ft. Despite the indifferent visibility, Belgrave soon spotted a German two-seater. It was a tempting target and he pushed his brown-painted SE5a into a dive on his intended victim. As the range rapidly closed, he squeezed the trigger levers on the control stick to unleash bursts of fire from his two machine-guns. Two of the Captain's comrades, who had stuck with their leader in his headlong descent, also joined the attack. Belgrave and his prey spiralled ever lower until both were swallowed by the low cloud shrouding the enemy-held countryside some four miles east of the battered French town of Albert. Details of what happened next are now as vague as shapes in the Somme mist that morning nearly 90 years ago but hunter and hunted smashed into the ground. Belgrave was killed, finally forsaken by the good fortune that had protected him in several brushes with death during nearly four years in uniform. He was 21.

The name of James Belgrave became one more to be absorbed into the hideous arithmetic of the Great War's casualty lists, his passing briefly noted then forgotten other than among grieving family, friends and closest comrades. Even in the 'glamorous' occupation of war flying, lasting fame was reserved for the few. Fate decreed that Belgrave's undoubted courage and dedication were not enough to earn him his place in legend alongside Albert Ball, Edward 'Mick' Mannock, James McCudden and a handful of others with great tallies of aerial victories and the highest awards for valour. Yet his story is well worth recording, not least because, as a member of a proud family of squires, country clerics and distinguished naval and military men, he typified the dutiful youth of his class who became the junior officers of the war and thus figured so prominently in the ranks of the so-called Lost Generation. Today the aces are long gone. No one who flew with Belgrave is left to tell first-hand what it was like to dice high in the icy air against the garishly painted Fokker and Albatros and watch as friend or foe plummeted to destruction in a spiral of flame and greasy black smoke. Also, few of Belgrave's letters have survived, so a fully rounded biography is not possible. But some of the officers who served with him did leave their memoirs or diaries and more can be gleaned from the terse commentary in flaking combat reports, service records and other papers. There emerges a story which echoes the tragedies of so many of the brave sons who were mourned in our sad shires.

# CHAPTER ONE

# BORN TO LEAD

IT seemed the best of times. When James Belgrave was born on September 27 1896 Victoria had reigned for 59 years. Although poverty and sweated toil were the lot of many of the old Queen's subjects, the notion of British invincibility went unquestioned by pauper and peer alike. The Empire had reached its zenith, protected by the mightiest navy the world had seen and policed by a volunteer Army which, though tiny by European standards, was deemed adequate to deal with any difficulties in the colonies. Certainly James Belgrave's parents, Dalrymple and Isabella, could reasonably expect prosperous and secure lives for their infant son and his brother Charles, born twenty-one months earlier. The couple, who were to have no other children, were comfortably placed socially and financially. They had married in January 1894 when Dalrymple, a well-travelled barrister-at-law, author and member of a long-established family of gentry, was 43. His bride was eleven years younger, an age gap not unusual for a couple of their time and class. Isabella was a daughter of the Richardson family, bankers and industrialists who had split from their Quaker roots earlier in the century.

Of course, the proud couple could not know that the simple fact of their sons being born in the mid-1890s guaranteed that they, like millions of other young men, would be drawn into the most cataclysmic conflict the world had seen. Class and education destined the brothers for service as junior officers in the Great War, with all the appalling risk that that implied. Chance ruled that Charles would emerge unscathed to forge a long and distinguished civilian career, culminating in a knighthood, while James would be decorated twice for courage only to die before his twenty-second birthday. However, on that breezy Sunday when James Belgrave was born at the family home in a smart, mid-Victorian terrace in Pitt Street, three minutes' stroll from Kensington Palace, there were few omens to disturb his mother and father's contentment. The Russian Tsar Nicholas and his wife Alexandra were being entertained by their British relations at Balmoral, where the young autocrat, along with the Prince of Wales, the Duke of Connaught and some thirty gillies, had already shot ten fine deer. Meanwhile Colonel Sir Horatio Herbert Kitchener, Sirdar or commander of the Army in Egypt, was quietly celebrating his promotion to Major-General. Who could have predicted that, as Earl Kitchener, Secretary of State for War, he would glare from countless posters summoning the youth of Britain to its fate – or that the Russian imperial couple and their five children were to be murdered in a dingy basement in a Urals mining town amid the turmoil wrought by the Great War?

All that was the unthinkable future as Dalrymple Belgrave penned a brief announcement of his second son's birth for inclusion in the following Tuesday's edition of *The Times*. Some five weeks later, on October 30, the Belgraves took the infant to be baptised at St Mary Abbots, the parish church round the corner from their home. The child was christened James Dacres Belgrave.

So who were the Belgraves? The family came of Norman stock. Their ancestors followed the Conqueror to England and established themselves at a village by an ancient crossing place on the Soar to the north of Leicester. In Domesday, the settlement was listed as Merdegrave, from the Old English *mearth graf* (martin's grove). Apparently the new Norman lords found the name distasteful, for in Old French *merde* meant filth, and that element of the name was soon dropped in favour of *bel* – beautiful. By 1135 the village was Belgrave, a name that survived the area's later development as a select suburb for well-to-do tradesmen and final engulfment in the scruffy urban sprawl of modern Leicester. Today some Belgrave family members are sceptical of the suggestion that their forebears simply took the place name as their own and favour the idea that the lords of Bellegrave, near Rouen in Normandy, brought the name with them at the time of the Conquest.

What is certain is that a William de Belgrave was given land in the area by Robert Blanchmaines, Earl of Leicester, in the second half of the 12th Century.

William's descendants prospered as influential landowners and churchmen and boasted at least one knight among their number – Sir George Belgrave, who clashed with the Earl of Huntingdon and found himself arraigned before the Star Chamber in 1601. An enthusiastic genealogist in the family even established a Belgrave line back to the Plantaganet King Edward III, albeit with some jinking through female links. The family's ties to their home village gradually faded and in the 14th Century Belgraves already owned land in North and South Kilworth in the south of Leicestershire. By the early 1500s the family held the manor of Nether Hall in North Kilworth and the village became home to the principal line of Belgraves, who took as their arms a silver chevron and three perforated lozenges on a red field with a ram's head as crest. The association of family and village endures today.

Although James Belgrave was London-born and an infrequent visitor to North Kilworth, that village close by the Avon in unspectacular, typical Midlands farmland is where his roots lay. At the time of his birth not only were the Belgraves among the area's principal landowners but every rector of North Kilworth for nearly two centuries had been a Belgrave. Other members of the family were clergymen in the neighbouring county of Rutland during the 18th and 19th Centuries. With four hundred acres of glebe in the parish of North Kilworth, the Belgrave parsons enjoyed a prestige and prosperity unknown to today's team ministers. One of the village's rectors was James Belgrave's great-grandfather Thomas, who held the living for forty-two years until he died out hunting in 1854. The clergyman's elder son, also Thomas and grandfather to James, joined the Royal Navy at 14 as a first-class volunteer. The boy sailor was soon aboard a warship helping to suppress the slave trade off West Africa and was in at the capture of a pirate schooner. Service in the tropics eventually wrecked Thomas's health and he died in his native Leicestershire at 41 but not before he had risen to commander and married into a distinguished naval family.

Thomas's wife Charlotte was a daughter of Vice-Admiral James Richard Dacres. During the War of 1812 Dacres was commanding the worn-out frigate Guerrière when he tangled with the American warship Constitution, the legendary Old Ironsides, seven hundred miles east of Boston. Hopelessly outgunned, he fought on until, badly wounded with a musket ball in the back and with his ship demasted and fifteen crew killed, he accepted that surrender was inevitable. It was to Dacres, his gallant great-grandfather, that James Belgrave owed his unusual second name. The custom of Belgrave sons being given the

Christian name Dacres is still followed. Further cementing the link between the two families, Commander Thomas Belgrave's younger brother Charles, a Royal Navy chaplain, married another of Admiral Dacres's daughters, Annie. Charles left the Navy in 1854 and became the fifth and final Belgrave to be Rector at North Kilworth, following his father and exceeding even his fine record by holding the living for forty-six years.

Surprisingly, neither of Commander Belgrave's sons was tempted to follow the naval tradition. The elder boy, the first Belgrave to be named Dacres, went into the Army after Eton. The second son, James's father Dalrymple, was also immune to the lure of the sea, despite being born at Portsea, almost in sight of the naval dockyards of Portsmouth. Dalrymple, whose Christian name honoured another distinguished relative in the Dacres family, was only six when his father died. He did sufficiently well at public school to earn a place at Trinity College, Cambridge, where he achieved a BA degree before opting for a career in law. He was called to the Bar when he was 26 and started accepting briefs for criminal cases in and around London. He was, however, a young man of independent mind and thought nothing of taking time out to cycle across the Continent, toting little more than cash, a pipe and tobacco pouch and with his toilet sponge tucked under his cap. In early 1880 his adventurous spirit took him to South Africa where he set up in legal practice in the diamond boom town of Kimberley and for a time shared a house with the buccaneering arch-imperialist Cecil Rhodes, founder of Rhodesia. Dalrymple's experiences provided him with a rich source of material when, after returning to England a few years later, he found time between court work to try his hand at writing and magazine editing. He won some acclaim for a book of short stories called *Luck At The Diamond Fields* about the characters he had encountered in the rough-and-tumble world of the Veldt's mining communities. Tales such as *A Vaal River Heiress* and *A Fatal Diamond* had one London reviewer enthusing that the author had 'hit upon an entirely new vein and has worked it most successfully'. Dalrymple's insight into the criminal mind inspired further books, including *A Great Turf Fraud: A Queer Story of the St Leger*, which was published as one of a series of popular 'shilling sporters'. During the early 1890s Dalrymple was a welcome guest at North Kilworth where his uncle Charles, the Rector, doubtless enjoyed some trusted male company as he had six spinster daughters and his only son had died aged four. Indeed, the old parson appointed his nephew as one of his executors.

It is unclear how Dalrymple met the gentlewoman who was to become his wife and mother of his two sons but Isabella Richardson certainly came from an intriguing background. Her forebears belonged to a network of Quaker entrepreneurs which, in the early 19th Century, was a driving force in the transformation of parts of the North East of England from an undeveloped backwater into a powerhouse of iron-making, engineering and other manufacturing enterprises. The Richardsons were linked by marriage and business to leading figures in the Society of Friends, such as the Gurneys, Peases, and particularly the Backhouses, key investors in ambitious projects including the Stockton and Darlington Railway, which opened in 1825. A Backhouse bank, founded in Darlington, thrived thanks to astute management and sound risk assessment, surviving several runs on its reserves. It established close ties with other banks run by Friends in Norwich and London until it became one of the main constituents of Barclays, the 'Quaker Bank' founded in 1896.

Isabella's grandfather, Jonathan Richardson, was given a head start in banking thanks to his mother having been a Backhouse before marriage. Unfortunately he did not inherit the financial acumen and probity associated with the name. Jonathan was made manager of a branch of the Backhouse bank in Newcastle and when it amalgamated with the Northumberland and Durham District Bank in 1836 he became managing director. At first the concern prospered and the ambitious banker developed a spa near his estate at Shotley Bridge, Co Durham, where visitors included the Duke of Wellington and Charles Dickens. Jonathan also leased mineral rights to Quaker cronies who ran the nearby iron works, which later became the huge Consett steel plant. Disastrously, he allowed his own interests and those of his friends to become hopelessly enmeshed with the bank's. The iron works' rapid expansion was financed by the bank, which lent a million pounds, a huge sum at the time, on the strength of promissory notes and a mortgage on the company's plant. Only Jonathan knew exactly how recklessly he was dicing with insolvency. A run on funds ruined the bank in 1857 and it took a frantic rescue operation by Quakers to save the iron works from a similar fate. The Society of Friends was deeply disturbed by the effect the crash had on its reputation for business integrity, not to mention the financial hardship caused to members who had stakes in the bank and works. It did not help that the banker and his son, Jonathan Backhouse Richardson, partner in a tin-plate manufacturing concern supplied by the iron works, seemed to have escaped from the shambles relatively unscathed financially. Richardson senior failed to demonstrate the penitence the local meeting of Friends deemed due and was disowned in 1858. His wife and most of his family resigned.

Isabella, the ninth of Jonathan Backhouse Richardson's eleven children, was born at Shotley Bridge in 1861. At that stage the Richardsons' severance from the Quakers was practically complete but enough of the family fortune remained intact for Isabella to be brought up in comfortable circumstances. By the time she met Dalrymple Belgrave in the 1890s her father had died and her mother Rachel was spending much of each year in Switzerland, living in an imposing mansion called Villa Victoria overlooking Lac Léman (Lake Geneva) at Clarens, a little to the west of Montreux. It is possible Dalrymple met his bride-to-be in Switzerland while he was touring Europe; or perhaps the couple were introduced while Dalrymple was engaged in court work in the North East of England at a time when the Richardsons were visiting family and old friends in the area. On January 4 1894 Dal and Bella were married in the Anglican church of St John the Evangelist at Territet on the eastern fringe of Montreux. The previous day the couple had taken the train along the lake to Lausanne for the necessary civil marriage formalities at the British vice-consulate. The newlyweds, with a maid in attendance, settled into a pattern of long stays in hotels in Montreux, broken up by return visits to London, a considerable but reasonably straightforward journey by train. In Switzerland, the Belgraves were not short of congenial company; at the time Territet was a fashionable haunt of well-to-do British and one was as likely to hear English spoken on the streets as French. Also, the couple were close to Isabella's older sister Marion and her husband Sherlock Willis, a retired Royal Scots major whom she had married at Territet two years earlier. Indeed, the Major was one of the witnesses at the Belgraves' wedding.

Isabella soon found she was expecting her first child and Marion, who already had a son of her own, was a welcome support for her sister. In December 1894 both couples established themselves at the Hotel-Pension Maison-Blanche in Montreux in preparation for the birth. Isabella had her first son on December 9 1894 and he was christened Charles Dalrymple Belgrave at St John's the following February. When mother and child were ready to travel, the family returned to England to show off the new arrival. The Belgraves stayed in Pitt Street at the house which Dalrymple's widowed mother Charlotte had taken a few years earlier. For Dalrymple it was an easy ride across town to his chambers in Fig Tree Court, Inner Temple, from where he accepted briefs for cases at the

Old Bailey and Sessions in London and Middlesex. Pitt Street was also handy for Kensington Gardens. It was there, while still in his pram, that Charles met his future wife Marjorie Barrett-Lennard. Their families had been friends for generations and Charles and Marjorie's mothers would meet for a stroll through the gardens with their children on the nurses' days off. Dalrymple kept the house on after his mother died in 1895 and when Isabella found she was expecting James the couple decided to stay in London for the birth. Charles and his new brother, nicknamed Carol and Jim by their family, were healthy youngsters and grew rapidly. Eventually both would easily top six feet, not surprising as their father was 6ft 4ins.

The family's visits to Switzerland continued into the 1900s. A favourite springtime outing for Isabella was to take her sons on the half-hour train ride from Montreux to the small town of Les Avants where, in the mountain meadows, the boys gathered armfuls of the narcissi for which the area is still noted. However, the new century had brought an increasingly ominous backdrop to such idyllic scenes. British complacency had been rattled by the Boer War, which had ended in victory in 1902 but not before the Mauser-wielding Dutch farmers had delivered some embarrassing, not to say lethal, lessons about tactics. Also the old yachting rivalry between Victoria's petulant grandson, the German Kaiser Wilhelm, and her son Bertie, by now King Edward VII, was about to displaced by an altogether more serious contest. The race to build Dreadnoughts at massive expense would heighten tensions between Britain and Germany in the countdown to Armageddon.

For the Belgraves there were also changes on the domestic front. In 1905 Isabella's mother, the only grandparent James had known, died. It was also time for the young brothers, who had been educated at home, to start public school. A more permanent move back to England was inevitable. Dalrymple's old school, Bedford Grammar, was the obvious choice for his sons. The relatively inexpensive education it offered and Bedford's air of gentility had helped make the town a magnet for professional and military families returning from the colonies, particularly India. The Belgraves took a double-fronted house in Merton Road, in an area where a late-Victorian development of homes had sprung up as a direct result of the influx of the Anglo-Indians. It meant that Charles and James had only a short walk across Kimbolton Road to one of the side gates of the school after they started as day boys on November 4 1905, entered on the register as 5559 Belgrave C D and 5560 Belgrave J D respectively. There was still an emphasis on classics in an establishment that prided itself on turning out boys who would be the clerics, diplomats and, particularly, members of the armed forces needed to provide the cement of empire. However, the school, which was to drop Grammar from its title in 1917, had seen much change since Dalrymple left in 1866. Dr John Edward King, who had been Head Master for two years when the Belgrave boys arrived, was a moderniser well attuned to the new century. Among his innovations was an engineering course taught in well-equipped workshops.

Nine-year-old James started lessons under Miss Skevington in form I iv of the preparatory school, known as the Inky. Not surprisingly, considering he had started midway through the term, James, or Belgrave (ii) as he was listed, came bottom of the class of twenty-seven boys, though he managed a creditable fourteenth place in French, doubtless helped by his days in Switzerland. James made steady if unspectacular progress through the school and by his early teen years he seemed to have set his sights on a military career. When the time came to specialise he entered the Civil and Military department, whose aim was to prepare boys for entry to what were then the Royal Military College at Sandhurst in Berkshire, for would-be cavalry and infantry officers, or the Royal Military Academy, Woolwich, for young men destined for the Royal Artillery or Royal Engineers. Although his father had shunned a life in uniform, James was not short of military influence from within the family. His uncle Dacres Belgrave, who by then held the family estate at North Kilworth, had retired from the Queen's Own Royal West Kent Regiment with the rank of Lieutenant Colonel. Dacres's elder son Hew had followed his father into the regiment and acquitted himself well in the Boer War when barely in his twenties. He, too, would rise to Colonel. Hew's younger brother John was making his way as an officer in the Royal Artillery, also after service in South Africa. Both of these cousins of James Belgrave would survive the Great War with a DSO apiece to their credit. James became a 1st Corporal in the school's cadet corps, which had been revitalised under Dr King. The Head took personal control of the corps, assuming the rank of Major, and even joined the boys in summer camp. His troops sported pillbox hats tilted at a rakish angle and on Empire Day, each May 24, there was never any shortage of heavily decorated Old Bedfordians to take the salute.

Bedford's pupils were given an astonishing insight into 20th Century technology when, on the evening of July 23 1913, an old boy, aviation pioneer Claude Grahame-White, landed his aeroplane on the playing field. Whether this sowed the seed of interest in aviation that eventually led to James Belgrave joining the Royal Flying Corps we do not know. Certainly there had rarely been such excitement at the school. Michael De-la-Noy, a pupil from a later generation, captured the scene admirably in his book *Bedford School: A History*. He told how Grahame-White, a 34-year-old aeronautical engineer who went on to win many flying prizes and to write extensively on aeronautics, was surrounded by crowds of sightseers as he stepped from his primitive aircraft. The aviator was welcomed by the Head Master, who presumably had been forewarned of the visit, and the machine was wheeled to the back of the school, where it was left overnight. The next morning many scholars made themselves late for lessons by pausing to gawp at the contraption, which stood under the guard of two local policemen. It was the first aeroplane many of the boys had ever seen, at close quarters at any rate, and at mid-morning they were treated to a talk from Grahame-White in the Great Hall. He then took off in his flimsy-looking machine, flew three times over the town and again landed on the playing field. It was reported that he had no sooner alighted than he was caught up on the shoulders of a crowd of boys and carried into the school. Michael De-la-Noy noted: 'For the boys, with the Great War and the advance in mechanisation that it was to foster only a year distant, their encounter with the intrepid airman and his innovative flying machine placed them at the very frontiers of the 20th Century.'

By the end of that year James Belgrave was seventh out of the eighteen boys in the Civil and Military sixth form under Mr A W Lucy, with English and French appearing to be his strongest subjects. He had made no great impact on the sports field during his time at Bedford but earned a place in the Second VIII rowing squad of 1913, reckoned one of the best teams of the era. In 1914, impatient to start his Army life, James seems to have found little motivation for lessons. That summer he ended his school days placed twelfth out of the fourteen boys in Mr J T Little's upper sixth form. But no matter, he had already passed Certificate A, the exam designed specifically for youngsters hoping for a commission. His application for admission to the Royal Military College was accepted although he owned up to having missed cadet camp through an infection.

At the end of June James declared to a medical board that he was fit for Army service and he stood on the threshold of his military career. By then war was inevitable, with Europe a powder keg of alliances and antagonism. When

Bedford School held its speech day on July 27 the fuse had already been lit by the assassination of Archduke Franz Ferdinand in Sarajevo a month previously. The school's guest of honour was Field Marshal Earl Roberts, the diminutive hero who had won the Victoria Cross with deft and deadly displays of his sword skills in the Indian Mutiny fifty-six years before. The old warhorse seized the opportunity to remind the boys of their duty to Country and Empire and called for the formation of a 'national army'. Eight days after his rousing speech the country was at war. Bobs died that November, blissfully ignorant of the toll that was to be exacted from the boys he had addressed with such conviction.

# CHAPTER TWO

# TO WAR

ALL over by Christmas! The chief concern of James Belgrave and thousands of eager young men like him was that they would have no chance to prove their mettle in uniform before the Kaiser was put firmly in his place and the whole show came to an end. Lord Kitchener's worries were somewhat different. He reckoned the war would last three years and need a million men. Even those calculations were to prove hopelessly optimistic, of course. After a sodden Bank Holiday weekend Britain declared war on Germany at 11pm on Tuesday August 4 1914. Ostensibly the reason was the violation of Belgian neutrality by German forces as they launched what was intended to be a rapid sweep on Paris, by-passing France's imposing eastern defences. However, outrage at the plight of 'plucky little Belgium' conveniently masked the British Government's determination that Germany should not be allowed to dominate Europe and snatch control of French ports from where its ships could menace the Channel.

The 64-year-old Kitchener, hastily recalled from Egypt to become Secretary of State for War, told the politicians what they did not want to hear: that any idea of a brisk war of manoeuvre lasting a few months was fanciful. He also understood better than anyone the daunting mathematics of the situation. Britain's regular Army comprised just seven available divisions, including one of cavalry, compared to Germany's ninety-eight and a half. Two days after assuming office Kitchener appealed for 100,000 volunteers, then another 100,000 and soon 300,000 men had enlisted in response to his proclamation

Your Country Needs You. The patriotic stampede to join the colours still left the formidable problem of selecting and training enough men of the right calibre to be the officers of the hugely expanded Army. Youngsters like James Belgrave with the social background and public school education usually perceived as necessary for an officer were at a premium.

In peacetime Belgrave would have expected to spend a year at the Royal Military College (later Academy) at Sandhurst before accepting a commission. However, having arrived there ten days after the outbreak of war, he was considered ready to join a regiment just four hectic months later. He was granted a prize cadetship and in any event his father would have been saved £150 as the standard Sandhurst fees were waived soon after war broke out. By the time Belgrave arrived at Sandhurst he had already set his sights on joining the Oxfordshire and Buckinghamshire Light Infantry. There were good reasons for his choice of regiment. James's aunt, Dalrymple's younger sister Mary, and her husband Eustace Mansel had a farm high on the ridge of the Chilterns above the Oxfordshire village of Chinnor. Before the war Dalrymple and his wife had taken up the Mansels' suggestion to become neighbours and moved to County End, a house which, as its name implied, was only yards from the Buckinghamshire border. Mansel, a magistrate aged 60 at the outbreak of war, had been a captain in the forerunner of the Ox & Bucks, the Oxfordshire Light Infantry. Originally the 52nd Regiment of Foot, it counted Waterloo among battle honours dating back to Quebec in 1759. Doubtless Marlborough-educated Captain Mansel, himself son of a colonel, regaled his military-minded nephew James with tales of battles in the Sudan and his time as a general's aide-de-camp in India. He was delighted when James opted to join the latest incarnation of his old regiment.

The Oxfordshire and Buckinghamshire Light Infantry had been formed in 1908 as part of the wholesale Army reforms resulting from the lessons of the Boer War. (Another result of the shake-up was the encouragement of local rifle clubs where at least some young men could be trained in the use of small arms in a country hostile to the idea of conscription. Captain Mansel was instrumental in setting up Chinnor Rifle Club. It thrived and many members joined the colours during the Great War.) James Belgrave was destined for the Ox & Bucks' 2nd Battalion which, harking back to its illustrious predecessors, always liked to be known as the 52nd. As he was settling into Sandhurst his future comrades had already quit their base at Albuhera Barracks in Aldershot to take their place in the

British Expeditionary Force. The 2nd Battalion sailed from Southampton on August 13 as part of the 5th Infantry Brigade, 2nd Division, I Corps and landed at Boulogne the following afternoon. It soon became obvious that the Kaiser's men were no pushover and the Ox & Bucks regulars found themselves caught up in the retreat from the Belgium town of Mons, emerging exhausted but relatively unscathed. Young Belgrave's impatience to get into action was only heightened by news of his chosen regiment's role in reversing the Germans' push towards Paris during the Battle of the Marne early in September. Then, while he was devoting his energies to learning tactics, military law, administration, weapons handling and drill, the Ox & Bucks was next hurled into the First Battle of Ypres, helping to prevent the capture of the Flanders town whose name would become synonymous with slaughter by the war's end.

On December 16 1914, less than three months after his 18th birthday, Belgrave passed out of Sandhurst. He was immediately welcomed into his regiment as an ensign, or second lieutenant. By then the Ox & Bucks had acquitted itself well against opponents as formidable as the Prussian Guard and earned a niche in history as part of the force dismissed by the Kaiser as a 'contemptible little army'. Naturally, Belgrave realised there was more to becoming an Ox & Bucks subaltern than getting kitted out at a military tailors and buckling on the regiment's own distinctive alternative to the Sam Browne belt, which shunned the usual diagonal shoulder strap in favour of two vertical straps. However, imposingly tall and with his dark hair slicked down in the style of the times, he certainly looked the part of a dashing officer in a reasonably smart regiment. He was first posted to the 3rd (Special Reserve) Battalion, which had moved from its base at Cowley Barracks, Oxford, to its war station in Portsmouth on the outbreak of hostilities. The Battalion's chief role was to train men and officers to become replacements in the two regular battalions serving overseas. As Belgrave waited to take his place at the Front he and other newcomers cheerfully found themselves being indoctrinated into the traditions held dear by the regiment.

With the arrival of 1915 Belgrave was becoming increasingly anxious to see action. However, a different kind of concern was starting to grip the civilian population as war casualty lists grew and hopes of a knockout blow against Germany proved vain. The unease which James's family naturally felt for his future safety was only heightened by sad news that reached Eustace Mansel. His sister Elizabeth – Kitty to her family – had earlier inherited a country estate at

Sulby, three miles east of North Kilworth and over the border in Northamptonshire. Eustace was a regular visitor before the war and was on hand when unmarried Kitty decided to sell up and move to London. Parts of the estate were still being sold off as war came and Eustace got to know his sister's efficient young agent Charles Wartnaby. Now Wartnaby, who had gone to France as a lieutenant in the Northamptonshire Yeomanry in November 1914, was dead at 28, shot near Béthune.

Finally, by the end of May 1915, Belgrave was on his way by train and Channel troop ship to the Front. At the time replacements were sorely needed by the 2nd Battalion. It had just been mauled in the Battle of Festubert, part of an operation demanded of the British by their French allies in a futile attempt to push back the Germans over the flat coal-mining country north of Lens and east of Béthune. Around midnight on May 15 the battalion was sent out in support of the 2nd Royal Inniskilling Fusiliers, who fought their way through heavy machine-gun fire to the German positions. Two lines of enemy breastworks were captured but the cost was out of proportion to the success. The Ox & Bucks sustained 395 casualties, twenty of them officers, before it was pulled out of the line. The offensive resulted in more than 16,000 British casualties in total. The recuperating battalion was bolstered by the arrival of 270 men and six officers from England. Newcomers and old sweats alike were billeted in relative comfort and safety behind the lines in cottages at Raimbert, 'a curious little mining village', according to Lieutenant Colonel A J F Eden, who had taken command of the battalion that February. But it was three days after the main influx of replacements when Belgrave caught up with the battalion on Monday May 31 along with his fellow second lieutenants A G Cardy and J G Grant. By then the battalion's brief rest was at an end and the troops had marched fourteen miles to take their place in the trenches again, this time at the mining village of Mazingarbe, roughly midway between Béthune and Lens and about five miles south of the area of its brave but costly attack.

At last Belgrave, nervously intent on proving his worth, was in the line. However, this was not the Western Front of popular perception. No scenes of flooded shell craters and weary Tommies struggling through knee-deep mud greeted the young subaltern. Belgrave's first impression was of cloying heat and the intolerable glare thrown up by the chalk that predominated in the area. He arrived at a very quiet spell when mosquitoes were as much of a nuisance as the half-hearted German shelling and occasional shots from snipers spying their chances. Nevertheless officers and men seemed in a high state of alert, no doubt partly due to a visit that day by the divisional commander. The Ox & Bucks had taken over a section of Front from France's 281st Regiment of Infantry, who left behind trenches cut deep into the chalk, with well-made machine-gun emplacements. There were also many, usually soundly constructed, dug-outs, particularly in the support trenches. Unfortunately, some parts of the fire trench had dangerously long stretches without traverses, the 'battlement' patterns normally dug into the line to contain the blast from well-aimed shells and to hinder the movement of enemy troops if they infiltrated the trench.

There was a good system of communications trenches connecting the firing and second lines but these were also worryingly straight and wide. However, the greatest problem with the positions, which even a newcomer like Belgrave could not fail to note, was that the German front line, anything from two to three hundred yards away, generally followed a crest higher than the British trenches. What was a topographical triviality in peacetime gave the enemy a crucial advantage in those flatlands when it came to observation and beating off any attack – as would soon be proved. A feature of the barren landscape were the crassiers, the slag heaps of coal mines, where observation posts and machine-gun nests were placed.

Belgrave was allocated to D Company in the centre of the regiment's section of trench. Cardy and Grant were placed with B and C Companies respectively. (An infantry battalion was divided into four companies, in this case designated A to D, each with five officers and about 240 men when up to strength. The company commander was a captain). Belgrave, put in charge of a platoon of about sixty men, struggled against the misgivings felt by any young new officer. At merely 18 would he have what it took to earn the respect of the men he had to lead, many of whom were older and more experienced than him? And when it came to battle would he possess the necessary courage and nerve to acquit himself well? With these questions still to be answered he was reassured to find that D Company was blessed with sound officers willing to impart helpful advice to a trench novice. Among them were two stalwarts who had arrived with the battalion in France the previous August. Lt Pierce Newton-King, still only 19, had been wounded at Langemarck in the October and had been back with the battalion only nine days. A colonel's son from Devon, he was a qualified interpreter in German and French. The other 'original', 2nd Lt G Field, was promoted from colour sergeant in November 1914. He had seen action in the retreat from Mons, and on the Marne and Aisne. 2nd Lt Shirley Minifie-Hawkins was also at pains to impress on Belgrave that, even at quiet spells, death was constantly ready to claim the unlucky or unwary. As if to prove the point, the battalion reported one killed and seven wounded on the day of the new officer's arrival.

Things became a little more dangerous on Belgrave's second day. A newly-arrived trench mortar battery started lobbing shells into the German lines that morning. Colonel Eden noted ruefully: 'They did some useful shooting but as their efforts usually bring some form of retaliation they are not at present very popular with the people in the front-line trenches.' Belgrave was still getting the measure of his new surroundings when, on the evening of June 2, the battalion was relieved by the 2nd Inniskillings and moved back to billets in the village of Philosophe as part of the brigade reserve. As well as being generally filthy, Philosophe was too close to the front lines for comfort. It was also surrounded by French guns, making it a prime target for German artillery. The Tommies were reluctant to move around in anything other than small groups in daylight for fear of attracting fire from the enemy, who could see practically everything that was going on. The period out of the lines at least provided an opportunity for an evening memorial service to be held. Belgrave learned that parts of the area were still relatively unscathed by war. Near Philosophe, a wealthy mine owner's chateau commandeered as a divisional HQ for the French still contained handsome furniture. The grass in its well laid-out grounds was also kept carefully mown, this despite the estate's twenty-strong complement of gardeners being cut back to twelve by the French army's need for men. British divisional staff officers visiting the chateau noted that their arrival often seemed the cue for considerably increased attention from the enemy. Colonel Eden rated the battalion's five days at Philosophe as irritating and valueless because the unpredictable shelling, which left one man dead and another wounded, meant virtually no training was carried out. He was glad when on June 7 the order came through to move into divisional reserve with the remainder of the brigade. After their relief arrived Belgrave and his company set out at 8.30pm on a tiring three-hour march back to Verquin where they flopped into billets. Officers found their accommodation very limited as the crowded village was already headquarters of the 47th (London) Division. Belgrave was no longer the new boy as 2nd Lt Cecil Hurst-Brown, a 21-year-old from London, joined D Company that day. The two took the opportunity to compare notes as they had passed out of Sandhurst at the same time.

The hot weather persisted during the battalion's week in Verquin and Belgrave was kept busy with training sessions, including some night work. This rotation between front-line positions and billets to the rear was a well-established routine. Contrary to myth, British soldiers on the Western Front were not left to fester in filthy, rat-infested trenches, unrelieved for weeks on end. A battalion could expect, on average, to spend just ten days a month in the firing line. True to form, at 8pm on June 15 the Ox & Bucks quit Verquin to make the five-mile march, east through Sailly Labourse, to relieve the King's Regiment in the right sector of the Vermelles section. A comfortable regimental HQ was soon established at Le Rutoire Farm. Officers and men alike were pleased to find that again their trenches, set amid cornfields, were deep and on the whole well made. On the left of the battalion's sector the enemy line was 250 yards away, increasing to five or six hundred yards on the right. The top brass reckoned this was too far away and the whole brigade was soon at work making a new trench a hundred yards in front. It was nerve-jarring work, even under cover of darkness. The men had to take supreme care not to clank their picks and shovels together as the noise could have invited enemy fire. However, despite the activity, there was practically no enemy shelling or sniping to claim casualties. The Ox & Bucks' snipers and observers, on the other hand, got in some excellent practice, especially between 5pm and 7pm when the evening light from the west favoured their work. Night patrols were also stepped up.

One of Belgrave's fellow officers found the system of trenches, modified by both French and British, 'a complete maze'. Wistfully, Lt C A Fowkes added: 'Corn growing on the banks gives them the appearance from within of deep Devonshire lanes while from the outside they are quite invisible. If one stands up (at a safe moment) the scene is a wonderful one, no sign of other trenches as they are all covered by the self-sown ripe corn. The whole country is divided up into patches of brilliant yellow, red and blue – corn which cannot be gathered in, poppies and cornflowers.' At this stage, 'home' for Belgrave was a well-constructed dug-out, shared with two or three other officers. A typical dug-out in that sector was protected by four or five feet of timber, topped by corrugated iron and earth. The interior, perhaps 14ft by 9ft and 7ft high, would have had a wooden floor, a couple of tables, chairs for each occupant, beds of a sort and a stove. Elegant touches such as papered walls, lace curtains, a bookcase and flower vases made of old shell cases were common.

Friday June 18 was ostensibly just another day in the trenches. However, Belgrave, like every officer and man in the regiment, had had the significance of the date drummed into him. It was the anniversary of Waterloo, the benchmark of glory for the 52nd, and every year in peacetime an elaborate regimental sports day was held to celebrate. With 1915 being the centenary of the battle, the battalion had no intention of letting the occasion pass unmarked, war or no war. Of course, nothing could be arranged until a move out of the front line was scheduled. The next day brought relief and a march to excellent billets at Labourse. As the men were kept occupied practising their skills with rifle and bomb (as a grenade was then more commonly known), the officers lost no time in organising the Waterloo Sports. Luck was with them. There was not too much military activity so vehicles could be dispatched to fetch supplies from nearby Béthune, the ancient seat of the Counts of Flanders which was an important British headquarters for most of the war.

Most importantly, a large, flat grass field ideal for the event was at hand opposite the farmhouse used as the officers' mess. The big show was fixed for Tuesday the 22nd. Mindful that the regiment was in the country of its Waterloo foes and anxious not to offend the neighbours, the officers avoided having a gaudy programme printed and contented themselves with having a few modest sheets run off on the orderly room hectograph, precursor of the photocopier. At the foot of the programme was a cautionary note: 'Should a hostile aeroplane appear a bugler will sound three Gs as a signal to take cover under the wall or trees'. The warning proved unnecessary. The Germans proved sufficiently sporting, or at least indifferent, to avoid disrupting the events, which included races of a mile, half-mile, 220 yards and 100 yards, tug-of-war, pack-fighting between teams of six, a dispatch riders' competition and a bomb-throwing contest – using dummies. It was a fine day with enough breeze to prevent the competitors overheating. To Belgrave's delight, his company's team of four men and a 'patient' won the stretcher-bearers' competition. Everything was run on the usual peacetime lines, with an hour's break for tea in the afternoon, when the men were treated to fruit, and cakes baked by Sergeant Hazel and his cooks in the village baker's oven. The officers had even secured a band, a rare treat in the war zone, courtesy of the London Field Ambulance. The battalion's former commander Colonel H R Davies, promoted Brigadier General to command 3rd Brigade, 1st Division, turned up, as did XI Corps Commander Lieutenant General R C B Haking. The whole event was rated a resounding success.

Next day it was back to war business as usual. After being reinforced by twenty-five new men the battalion marched away to the village of Vermelles, still as part of the brigade reserve. Belgrave, whose first three weeks with the battalion had coincided with the relatively quiet spell, was soon given a taste of just how perilous things could be, even in billets away from the firing line. Four days after the Ox & Bucks' arrival in the village four men were wounded as German artillery targeted the area around the village church. Next day the shelling was stepped up and one man died and another eight were wounded when one shell blasted apart a house.

The battalion was glad to get away from the danger and grubby billets of Vermelles when the order was given that evening to march the six and a half miles to Béthune where rather safer and more comfortable accommodation was waiting in a former girls' school. The 'holiday' was short-lived, however. On June 30 the battalion took over a section of the front-line trenches from the 2nd Border Regiment at Givenchy, three miles north of their earlier trench positions and at a location where the line straddled the La Bassée canal. At one spot the enemy line was only fifty yards away. There was intermittent shelling over the next few days with two men killed and one wounded. For the next couple of weeks the battalion continued working the rotation in and out of the trenches at Givenchy with usually nothing more than the odd shell or rifle grenade in the front trenches to disturb another fairly quiet period, although two officers were wounded. Belgrave was saddened when, on July 11, his friend Minifie-Hawkins was badly injured by a trench mortar. A welcome move back to billets in Béthune on July 14 brought a period of relaxation interspersed with route marches, training in bomb-throwing and sessions on the rifle range. A brigade swimming competition in the town's public baths helped break the routine. It was a particularly welcome diversion for troops who often found themselves emerging hot, sticky and dirty from the trenches only to be accommodated in some stinking, fly-ridden farm building where they were able to take a bath once a week at best. On July 21 the battalion relieved the 3rd Coldstream Guards in the trenches at Cuinchy, south of the La Bassée canal. The Ox & Bucks had been in the same sector in March and older hands found the set-up pretty much the way they remembered it. Three companies were kept in the trenches while a fourth was held in reserve in a rear trench named Harley Street. The regimental HQ was in 'Woburn Abbey', a reconstructed house whose walls were decorated with pictures cut from the *Sketch* and other illustrated papers. The key feature of this stretch of Front was the brickstacks produced by the local works and providing a ready-made source of cover and strongpoints for the Germans. However, Belgrave had no time to become acquainted with the layout. Within a day of the battalion's arrival he was seconded for duty at corps headquarters. He had obviously impressed someone who thought it would be useful for the young officer to gain an insight into staff work. Belgrave's two-month 'apprenticeship' at the Front had gone well, transforming a lanky schoolboy into a useful and confident soldier. If not exactly a battle-seasoned veteran, he could be quietly satisfied with the way he had acquitted himself.

During Belgrave's absence the battalion was locked into its usual round of trench duty, often near Givenchy, and spells in reserve. Mosquitoes were still proving an irritation as the weather remained very hot. At least it meant that, when in the front line, the soldiers could lounge and snooze on the warm firestep as long as there was someone to take turn as lookout and gaze across no man's land through the trench periscope poked above the sandbags. Although the section of Front was still considered quiet the toll from shelling, trench mortars and the odd rifle grenade mounted inexorably. By the time the Ox & Bucks had been in France a year the number of casualties suffered by the battalion had exceeded its strength when it crossed the Channel. True, many of the 291 killed and 845 wounded were victims of the heavy fighting early in 1915 but the figures did not even take into account losses through sickness and other causes. On August 13, the anniversary of the battalion's sailing from Southampton, Colonel Eden calculated that of those who had embarked that day, there remained with the regiment seven officers, three warrant officers, twenty-seven sergeants, four buglers and 228 rank and file. Some officers suggested an anniversary dinner at Béthune's Hotel de France, which had remained open except for a couple of days at a time when the town was shelled. Colonel Eden was dubious about the celebration plans considering how the regiment had suffered but was persuaded at the last moment to attend. He would have had even less appetite for dinner had he known of the renewed suffering in store for his battalion.

Then, on August 16, the Ox & Bucks was sent into trenches in the left sector at Givenchy, a spot considerably more dangerous than those previously occupied. Two of the four companies were in the front-line trenches where craters caused by mining from both sides scarred no man's land. Three saps – small trenches dug forward of the main front line – reached to the lip of one crater as close as thirty yards from the Germans. The battalion hurled an average of two hundred bombs a night at the enemy, not really in the hope of reaching their trenches but to keep patrols from creeping over to the saps. Both sides also let loose with trench mortars and kept up a frantic digging of tunnels in attempts to lay mines to blow up the other's lines.

A much-needed, two-day rest in billets at Le Quesnoy was followed by more action for the Ox & Bucks. Things were hotting up. The enemy launched an attack just before midnight on August 26 and got close enough to hurl bombs into the saps, killing seven and wounding fourteen. It was a 'regular to do', as one officer related in a letter. But the Ox & Bucks' own bombers held firm, with men instantly replacing any casualties until the attack petered out at around 3am. The casualties were among a total of thirteen killed and twenty wounded in the battalion in the course of four days.

Belgrave was still away in early September when it was becoming obvious to the lowliest private that a Big Push was imminent. Officers were summoned to conferences, heavy guns were being moved closer to the Front and much emphasis was put on bombing practice. The Ox & Bucks was about to be thrust into the British Army's largest and costliest offensive to date. The object was a breakthrough to end the stalemate on the Western Front and perhaps even lead to an early end to the war. In that respect, what became known as the Battle of Loos, after the mining town whose capture was one of the key objectives, was a costly failure. Loos was also notable as the first time the British used poison gas against an enemy. The Germans had been denounced by the civilised world for using gas six months earlier at Ypres but the Allies reasoned that the game was now one of tit for tat. With just over a fortnight to go to the battle, the Ox & Bucks found itself back in billets at Le Quesnoy, supplying men for the job of bringing up the gas cylinders ready for the attack. The operation was supposed to be hush-hush and the gas was never referred to as such but was dubbed 'the accessory'. The cylinders were carried by rail to within a mile of the village, then had to be manhandled under cover of darkness to a rendezvous two miles from the front trenches, no mean feat. Each cylinder, nicknamed a 'rat', contained liquified chlorine gas, was about 6ft high and weighed about 160lbs. Two men carried the awkward load between them and with the frequent rest breaks required it could take as much as four hours to cover the distance. To give an idea of the scale of the task, the Ox & Bucks soldiers were among eight thousand men needed to get a total of more than five thousand cylinders into position for the whole attack as silently and carefully as possible.

The battalion received reinforcements of eighty-five men before going back into the trenches at Givenchy to relieve the 1st Queen's. It was while there that the officers received a reminder, if such a reminder were needed, of how a moment's inattention could spell death. At about 6am on September 8 Colonel Eden took two officers into a sap-head to examine the results of a mine the battalion had exploded an hour before. The three were congratulating themselves that the blast had removed the debris left by a German mine which had exploded the previous day, obstructing the view from the British trenches. Suddenly, Captain Ashley Ponsonby slumped across the Colonel, shot dead through the head by a sniper. The officers had believed they were under cover and that the light was too dim anyway for them to be targets. Ponsonby, at 34 one of the regiment's most popular officers, was from a distinguished family in Woodstock, Oxfordshire. A fine horseman, he had been giving riding lessons to some of the junior officers. It was perhaps some small tribute to him that, when back in reserve at Le Quesnoy, the battalion managed to stage a rough and ready steeplechase with twelve starters. The event, on September 18, was the last opportunity for such a diversion before Loos. On the next day the battalion relieved the 2nd Worcesters in the Givenchy trenches where sixteen machine-gunners and signallers joined as reinforcements. There was little action before the Worcesters returned on September 21, allowing the battalion to go back to Le Quesnoy.

That day Belgrave rejoined D Company, now under the command of Captain J A Southey, and was briefed on the regiment's role in the forthcoming action and his own duties as a platoon commander. His return was greeted by the start of the British artillery bombardment that would last ninety-six hours in an attempt to pulverise the German defences, or at least blast holes through the enemy wire, before the infantry launched their attack. The barrage, although puny by comparison with those in later battles, was the heaviest of the war so far. Belgrave, now facing by far his greatest test to date, was pleased to see that his fellow officers and the men were confident and in good spirits. As preparations for the attack continued on the following day, he was further encouraged to find that the barrage did not trigger retaliation from the German guns.

Then the weather broke. Heavy rain drenched the battalion on Thursday September 23 as a final reinforcement of sixteen machine-gunners and signallers arrived. That afternoon the Ox & Bucks trudged one final time to its old trenches at Givenchy to relieve the Worcesters. Belgrave, in common with the rest of the battalion, knew its next move would be 'over the top' to face the enemy at last. That night a thunderstorm provided an ominous backdrop to the sound of the 110 heavy guns and eighty-four other guns and howitzers relentlessly pounding away at the Germans. In the late afternoon of Friday, eve of the attack, the battalion took up battle stations. Special gas companies from the Royal Engineers moved into the front-line trenches to check the cylinders and attach the pipes intended to disperse the gas in the direction of the enemy lines. By midnight rain was pelting down.

It is outside the scope of this book to examine the battle in detail or analyse the results. General Sir John French, Commander-in-Chief of the British Expeditionary Force, had taken stock of the flat, open terrain beforehand and recognised that infantry advancing over such a landscape against machine-guns in entrenched positions were doomed to suffer heavy casualties. General Sir Douglas Haig, whose 1st Army was to mount the attack, had the same misgivings. Both generals also realised that, no matter how awe-inspiring the artillery barrage may be for the men in the trenches, the British had neither sufficient guns nor ammunition to guarantee success. The grandiose plan had been dreamed up by the French, who were to attack further south. Kitchener, anxious to maintain the Entente Cordiale, ordered the generals to go ahead. Haig put six divisions into the front line for the main assault on a front about six miles long, stretching from around Givenchy in the north to the suburbs of Lens in the south. There were to be diversionary attacks at each end of the line. Two divisions in reserve were supposed to exploit any gains made by the troops in the first wave. It was all an awful gamble and much hinged on the gas having the desired effect of panicking and disabling the German defenders.

James Belgrave found himself in the front line to the extreme left, or northern, boundary of the main attack. It worked out like this: the 2nd Division, commanded by Major General H S Horne, was positioned astride the La Bassée canal. Its main task was to form a flank guard to cover the major assault further south. It had been allocated a section about two miles long. The 5th Brigade, under Brigadier General C E Cochrane, was one of the division's three brigades and was dug in to the north of the canal and east of Givenchy. It was to launch a diversionary attack and so would go into action thirty minutes before the main thrust by units further south. Despite this subsidiary role the brigade had objectives: its orders were to take the enemy trenches opposite Givenchy and advance about half a mile to a line between the villages of Chapelle St Roch and

Cantaleux. In the brigade's section of line the Ox & Bucks was sandwiched between the 1st Queen's on the right and Territorials of the 7th King's Regiment to the left. Finally Belgrave's D Company was in the left of the regiment's sector with B Company in reserve. To the right was A Company, supported by C Company. The two front-line companies were established between Berkeley Street trench, about a hundred yards south of a feature known as The Shrine, to a position at the north end of a group of sizeable craters. In most of this area the British and German front lines were less than one hundred yards apart. D Company was under Captain Southey whose junior officers, apart from Belgrave, were Lt Newton-King, 2nd Lt Field and 2nd Lt Hurst-Brown. Instructions from corps level meant that only twenty officers from the battalion were to go into action. So D Company's 2nd Lt K Peploe, who had joined the battalion only the previous month, was among the officers left behind with reserve troops at Windy Corner, a position at a crossroads 1,500 yards behind the front line. The regimental headquarters had already moved into deep and fearfully cramped dugouts behind the support trenches.

In the early hours Belgrave and his fellow officers received word that the gas cylinders would be opened at 5.50am. The 5th Brigade's attack was to be launched at 6am. Commanders had been told that success depended on the advance being pushed with the 'utmost rapidity' to take advantage of surprise. Nerves and the wet weather made sleep next to impossible in the sodden trenches. As the night wore on Belgrave and other junior officers occupied themselves by ensuring that every man knew what was expected of him and had all his gear in place. Each soldier carried two hundred rounds of ammunition and two empty sandbags, an iron ration and extra cheese ration. Packs, including water-proof coats, were left stored. A haversack was carried on the back, with a waterproof sheet and cardigan waistcoat rolled on the belt below. Crucially, each man had a smoke helmet, supposedly proof against the gas and also the smoke that was to be released in the hope of covering the troops as they clambered out of the trenches. The helmet was a simple bag of flannel shirting worn tucked into the collar of the tunic and had a 'window' of transparent mica. This was difficult to see through, prone to crack and admit fumes, and the helmet itself was suffocating after a few minutes. The troops were told to keep the fronts of the hoods rolled up to the last minute but the rain caused the chemicals in the cloth to run and irritated the eyes. Improved respirators with glass eyepieces had yet to be issued to the Ox & Bucks. So that the men could recognise who was who under the helmets, everyone wore distinguishing marks sewn on to the upper part of the left arm. Each company commander wore a large letter, platoon commanders such as Belgrave and sergeants sported a large number and other ranks a small number. Orderlies wore a red and white band on one arm while the CO and adjutant had a small piece of regimental ribbon pinned on the shoulder. Men with Vermorel sprayers, devices like large garden insect sprayers, were ready to spread a solution to neutralise any chlorine lingering in the trenches. These men wore specially coloured armbands with the initials VS in case they were mistaken for deserters if found in a seemingly empty trench. The troops were warned not to consume any food or drink they found in German trenches because it would be contaminated by gas. Every minute officers anxiously monitored the wind direction and strength, vital factors if the gas attack were to succeed. Worryingly, the wind refused to stay in the desired quarter.

As the fateful hour approached the first streak of dawn appeared behind the German lines and the rain eased off. While the officers uttered final encouraging words to their men, about 150 tons of the greenish-yellow gas, only about half of the amount required to be really effective, was discharged along the whole length of front. The smoke candles were also lit. However, the wind had dropped and was barely enough to carry the gas towards the German trenches and even then it was not thick enough to bother the enemy unduly. The hoped-for German panic failed to materialise and the dreaded rattle of enemy machine-gun fire struck up and artillery shells started to fall in and around the trenches. At 5.58am a mine was exploded in the hope of rattling the Germans. Then two minutes later the men of the Ox & Bucks, bayonets fixed, jostled towards the ladders in the packed trenches, clambered over the parapet and set off into no man's land – and a nightmare. In their sector the wind was practically motionless or even blew the gas and smoke back towards them. Gas leaking from cylinder and pipe connections added to the problem. D Company suffered the worst. As the men advanced from their starting point, The Warren, they found themselves sweating in their masks, hardly able to breathe or see. Some raised the edge of the flannel in an attempt to breathe and caught a whiff of gas, rendering them helpless as they staggered and vomited in a frantic search for fresh air. Those unaffected gamely advanced on the craters in front of them, only to be met by withering machine-gun fire from Germans carefully dug in and untroubled by the gas. Enemy shells dubbed whiz-bangs by the Tommies seemed to be exploding everywhere. D Company went forward in two parties, each of two sections.

Newton-King, temporarily promoted Captain, led the southern party of about thirty men in a valiant attempt to outflank the craters. As the men rounded one corner of a crater's edge practically the whole group, including Newton-King, was wiped out in a hail of machine-gun fire.

The northern party made it to the edge of the craters and no further. The men succeeded in killing many Germans with rifle fire and bombs but could make no ground. There was too much wire intact in front of the enemy trenches and the German machine-gunners were too many and too well-prepared. To make matters worse, many of the British bombs proved dud. Match-style strikers used to set their fuses failed to work in the damp. In any case the bombs were incredibly dangerous to use. One Ox & Bucks man had blown himself to pieces the previous month when the bomb he was demonstrating to a comrade exploded just before he could throw it. The German bombs had handles and could be hurled much further, making it an uneven contest. The British Mills bomb, with its trademark pineapple shape and reliable lever action, was only just coming into service.

Amid the deadly chaos, Belgrave's first real taste of action was almost his last. Moments after climbing out of his trench he was caught by the blast of a high-explosive shell. Dozens of tiny fragments of metal and dirt peppered the right side of his face and he was left half-buried by earth thrown up by the explosion. Barely conscious and deafened in his right ear, Belgrave started choking on the gas that was still blowing back. His smoke hood had been partly blown off. Fortunately he was rescued without delay and bundled off to the regimental aid post as his comrades continued their courageous but futile attack. It seems likely he was passed on to an advanced dressing station at a spot called Lone Farm before a motor ambulance took him to a main dressing station somewhere around Béthune. 2nd Lt Field had also been caught out by the gas but gamely carried on. He survived the action and went on to win the Military Cross the following year. Hurst-Brown, however, was badly wounded and died next day. To the right of this disaster, A Company had things much better, at least at first. It experienced little difficulty in crossing the hundred yards or so to the German first line and many men even reached the second line thirty yards beyond. But within an hour the Germans hit back with bomb attacks and C Company, struggling under ferocious artillery fire, was unable to make much headway to help. The commander of A Company, Captain R M Owen, did not realise the two regiments on his right had already retired and his men were out on their own. They ran out of bombs but luckily found some German ones; when they too were expended Captain Owen gave the order to retire. 'God knows how I escaped,' he commented later. By 11am the Ox & Bucks and its neighbouring units were back in their own front line and enduring a steady bombardment of German shells. There was no attempt to renew the attack. The 5th Brigade had been told not to press on if its first efforts proved unsuccessful.

Meanwhile further south British troops captured eight thousand yards of German trenches and in places penetrated up to two miles, even taking the formidable strongpoint the Hohenzollern Redoubt. But the reserves were too tired and too far behind the battle front to move in to exploit the successes and fend off German counter-attacks. The large-scale breakthrough didn't happen. The Ox & Bucks casualties – killed, wounded, missing and gassed – on September 25 totalled eight officers, four of whom died, and 270 other ranks. The subdued and depleted battalion spent the next three very wet but fairly quiet days and nights in their trenches before being relieved by the Seaforth Highlanders and trudging thankfully to billets in Béthune. By then Belgrave was back in England. He had soon been identified as a 'Blighty' case and was taken from Béthune by train the eighty miles to Dieppe. On September 27, two days after his brush with death, he was put aboard the Stadt Amsterdam with other casualties for the trip across the Channel. The ship berthed at Dover the same day. It was James Belgrave's 19th birthday. Faint, prone to bouts of breathlessness and severely shocked by his ordeal, he was taken up to London where, three days later, he faced an Army medical board. The doctors found he was still slightly deaf and suffering a discharge from his damaged ear. His face wounds had also turned septic but youth and good health were on his side and both conditions would soon clear up. He was marked down as unfit for general service for two months and sent on sick leave. The Belgrave home amid the fields and beech woods of Chinnor Hill was an ideal spot for James to recuperate and reflect on the events of the Battle of Loos as it stuttered to a halt in mid-October with only minor gains, achieved at a cost of 61,713 British casualties. The blame for the failure was laid at French's door and he would be forced to resign that December.

James found that even rural Oxfordshire could not offer a complete haven from reminders of the war. His uncle Eustace Mansel, anxious to do his bit but barred from active service by age and failing health, had helped raise a local platoon for the Volunteer Defence Corps, an early version of Dad's Army formed for home defence duties. Mansel gathered recruits from Chinnor Hill and nearby Radnage and Bledlow Ridge. Even James's father Dalrymple, by now in his mid-60s, donned the blue-grey uniform. The volunteers sported arm bands bearing the royal initials GR, prompting jokes about George's Relics and Grandpa's Regiment. However, when age restrictions and medical fitness standards were later eased to fill gaps in the ranks of the regular Army, some members of the volunteer corps went to war and acquitted themselves well. The corps eventually became volunteer battalions of the Ox & Bucks.

James's elder brother was not at Chinnor to greet his arrival. Charles Belgrave, who never previously entertained the idea of joining the Army, had nevertheless felt the call of duty and cut short his studies at Oxford, where he had joined the Officers' Training Corps, to take a commission in the Royal Warwickshire Regiment. By the time James reached home Charles was in the Sudan. He would serve in various camel corps there and in Egypt and Palestine as Britain sought to protected her interests, and particularly the Suez Canal, against possible Turkish and German interference. Charles was involved in an expedition against the troublesome Sultan of Darfur – a 'somewhat Kipling-esque affair', he wryly recalled. In November, James wrote to the War Office reminding them that his sick leave was up. He was sent for a medical board at the 3rd Southern General Hospital in Oxford. Chinnor's railway station on a branch line of the Great Western made travel to this and later appointments relatively easy. Belgrave was still left breathless and faint by anything more than ordinary exertion and took with him a certificate from his own family doctor, who thought him unfit to return to active duty. The Army medics agreed and gave him two months more leave.

The old year had one last blow in store for the Belgrave family. On the last night of 1915 Eustace Mansel died at home, aged 62. It was decided that the Captain should be buried at North Kilworth where so many of his widow's Belgrave relatives lay. It was also close to his brother Ernest's grave at Sibbertoft. Ernest, who had died in 1911, and a third brother George – both retired officers like Eustace – were familiar figures with the Pytchley Hunt during winters earlier in the century when their sister Kitty was still at Sulby. Captain Mansel's coffin, with the Union Flag draped over it, was escorted from the house at Chinnor by his platoon of volunteers on the morning of January 5. It was then borne by motor hearse to Kilworth where the Ox & Bucks had sent four buglers to sound the Last Post at the funeral. A muffled peal sounded from the church bells at Kilworth that evening. James Belgrave was unable to attend his uncle's funeral because he had been summoned that day to another medical board. It was held at Portsmouth where he was nominally under the command of the 3rd Reserve Battalion. The examiners noted that his face wounds had completely healed but that the hearing in the right ear was still impaired to the extent that he could not hear a watch ticking at more than six inches away. He was still suffering from the effects of shock caused by the explosion and looked anaemic and weak. He told the doctors he was still prone to becoming breathless, faint and giddy. At 19, Belgrave was still growing fast and tired easily. He was unlikely to be ready for general service for four months. The doctors passed him fit for home service and light duties but this proved academic as he was sent off on leave until April anyway.

The arrival of 1916 had brought yet more sad news from the war. James's 31-year-old cousin Viola, daughter of his uncle Dacres, received word that her fiancé, Captain Gerald Fitzgerald of the 15th Battalion Durham Light Infantry, had been killed by a shell burst near Armentières on December 30. Harrow and Cambridge-educated Fitzgerald, aged 32, who had been wounded at Loos the day after James, was a barrister in civilian life. Viola, who had enrolled as a VAD (Voluntary Aid Detachment) nurse in 1914, went on to serve in France. She never married yet her family and that of her fiancé were nevertheless destined to be united. Captain Fitzgerald's mother was a Barrett-Lennard by birth and, as we have seen, James's brother Charles was to marry into that family, long-standing friends of the Belgraves.

James's health steadily improved and he was gratified when, on February 13, he was promoted Lieutenant. He knew it was only a matter of time before he returned to the war and indeed, a medical board at Oxford on April 3 passed him fit for general service as all symptoms from the gas poisoning had cleared up. However, the doctors agreed that the cumulative effects of his injuries had been very severe and on the strength of that Belgrave applied for a wound gratuity. He was awarded £125, a welcome sum for a young man who had existed on a subaltern's pay of 7s 6d (37p) a day. The need for officers at the Front was pressing and Belgrave was at Cambridge Barracks, Portsmouth, only briefly before being sent back to France. He rejoined the 2nd Battalion on June 2. It was glorious summer weather, a reminder to Belgrave of the day just over a year before when he first arrived at the Front. Many of the faces from that time had gone but Belgrave did not feel a stranger in his own battalion because he had travelled back to the trenches in the company of Captain Aubrey Carew-Hunt, Lt P L C Webster and Lt F W C Chippindale who, like him, had been recovering from wounds. Carew-Hunt, of A Company and Webster, of C Company, had both been injured on the same day as Belgrave during the ill-fated attack from Givenchy. The evening of the officers' return saw the battalion moving into trenches at Vimy Ridge ten miles south of the scene of their previous exploits. It proved a quiet night and Belgrave and the other new arrivals were kept busy overseeing men repairing the trenches. The next day it became apparent that much hard work was needed on deepening and connecting up the trenches. It was practically a new line some three or four hundred yards in the rear of the former British positions from where the 47th Division had been driven back twelve days previously. Heavy shell fire interfered with the work for a couple of hours.

As the men continued their toils word arrived on June 4 of the Battle of Jutland three days previously, the reports making it clear that both the British and German fleets had suffered heavy losses in their North Sea encounter. The following night the battalion suffered an individual loss of its own when Carew-Hunt was killed. He climbed out of a sap-head at 10pm before it was fully dark and was shot, dying a few minutes later. The 24-year-old clergyman's son came from Tiddington, about seven miles west of Belgrave's home village Chinnor. On June 6 the battalion was relieved and sent back into support positions in three redoubts. The following day brought more grim news. Lord Kitchener had drowned when the cruiser Hampshire taking him to Russia was sunk by a German submarine in the North Sea.

Conditions in the redoubts were crowded and dirty but there was little activity so Belgrave was at least able to get a bath and good night's rest as three or four officers at a time were allowed back to the comparative comfort of the village of Petit Servins. On June 10 the battalion was back in the trenches. It was still quiet, certainly at night, because both sides were far too busy working on their defences to want to interfere with one another. The arduous and tricky work of constructing deep dug-outs in the front-line system continued apace. As the month progressed the battalion moved back into cramped billets at Estrée-Cauchée where a nearby range allowed each company to get in some rapid-firing practice. Such mundane infantry matters would soon cease to be of direct concern to Belgrave. He was off to join the Royal Flying Corps. What persuaded him to seek the transfer we do not know. It was hardly the prospect of a safer life; enough infantrymen had witnessed the ghastly spectacle of fliers crashing to earth engulfed by the petrol-fuelled flames of their stricken aircraft. Certainly there was much appeal in the promise of comfortable quarters ten or fifteen miles behind the lines, away from the rat-infested and sometimes sodden trenches. Perhaps it was the memory of Grahame-White landing on the school field at Bedford or a chance encounter with an enthusiastic RFC officer that prompted Belgrave to seek a new direction in his military career.

Most probably the deciding factor was the determination to make a more notable and individual contribution to the war effort. There was the notion of a pilot being somehow special, above the earthbound masses, perhaps more in control of his own destiny than was possible for a subaltern huddling anonymously in some trench, impotent against enemy shelling. Whatever the reason, Belgrave went home in July to a country reeling from the enormity of the losses at the opening of the Battle of the Somme on the first day of that month. The catastrophe had cost 60,000 casualties, 20,000 of them deaths, on the blackest day for the British Army before or since. For Belgrave it was some consolation that his battalion, still near Vimy to the north of the battle, had been spared. And the regret he felt at leaving behind comrades with whom he had shared so much was soon to fade amid the exciting novelty and challenge of flying training.

**James Dacres Belgrave after he was awarded the Military Cross in 1917**

**Elder brother Charles in 1913**

**Reverend Charles Belgrave**

**Eustace Mansel, James's uncle**

**Dalrymple J Belgrave, father**

**Young Charles and James Belgrave gathering narcissi at Les Avants**

**Villa Victoria (left foreground) where James's grandmother lived**

**Merton Road
in Bedford**

**Birthplace in Pitt Street**

**County End at Chinnor**

James Belgrave (front row third from right) at Bedford Grammar School shortly before the Great War

**James and Charles Belgrave with a chum called Hayman early in the war**

**Belgrave on leave at Le Touquet**

**Dalrymple in Bucks Volunteers**

# COMBATS IN THE AIR.

Squadron : 45

Date : 24th

Type and No. of Aeroplane : A/1071

Time : ~~12~~ 11-15 a.m.

Armament : 1 Vickers Gun 1 Lewis Gun

Duty : ~~Defensive~~ Defensive Patrol

Pilot : Lut Belgrave

Height : 10,000

Observer : Sub Lieut Thompson

Locality : N.E. of Ypres

**Remarks on Hostile Machine :—Type, armament, speed, etc.**

The H A was a tractor - Coloured white, with
several black stripes at each side of the black cr

---

## Narrative.

we met

N.E of Ypres, a H.A. flying S.W. Seeing our
formation he turned S.E, & dived for the ground.
We dived after him flying E, & opened fire wi
the pilots gun. The H.A however was diving
at a greater speed - & was at a considera
distance. My engine became choked, and ~~afte~~
for some time firing intermittently - & then cut
out altogether. We then glided ~~eastwards~~ westwards & lan
on No 42 Squadron's aerodrome at Bailleul.

James Belgrave's first combat report while with No 45 Squadron in 1916

Belgrave (second from right) in 1917 with Vessey (third from left), Fitchat (fourth from left) and Austin (far right)

Belgrave (right) at Ste-Marie-Cappel airfield in 1917 with (from left) Austin, Truscott and unknown

Sopwith Strutter A1114 of the type flown by Belgrave with No 28 and No 45 Squadrons

**James Belgrave at Ste-Marie-Cappel during the perilous days of 1917**

**Belgrave at No 61 with (from left) Thompson, Hutcheon and Macvicker**

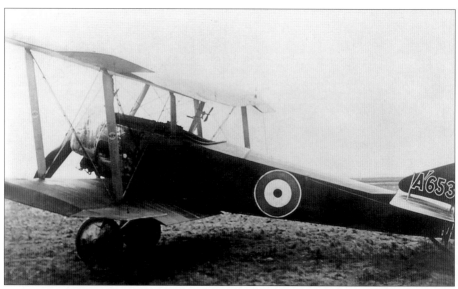

**Sopwith Pup A653, the aircraft in which Belgrave crashed at low-level**

**SE5a of No 61 (HD) Squadron where Belgrave flew on home defence**

**The memorial to James Belgrave in St Andrew's church, North Kilworth**

**James Belgrave's headstone in Grove Town Cemetery, near Albert**

# CHAPTER THREE

# AD ASTRA

THEY called them Huns. The Royal Flying Corps' pupil pilots were so prone to bending and breaking aircraft that exasperated instructors cynically reckoned that they might as well be Germans because of the damage they were inflicting on the Allied war effort. In their turn, the instructors, many of them exhausted and nervy fliers sent back from combat for a rest, often lacked the patience and calm teaching skills necessary for the job. In truth, at the time James Belgrave opted for the RFC, recruitment procedures and instruction were laughably rudimentary. A young officer seeking selection was likely to be asked if he rode to hounds, the logic being that a good 'seat', natural balance and sensitive hands were precisely the qualities required for the cavalry of the sky. Belgrave had no particular enthusiasm for the chase but trotted out enough satisfactory answers to questions about his riding ability, knowledge of mechanics and internal combustion engines and his interest in aviation to be accepted for training. Eyesight tests were just as perfunctory. A candidate's colour vision was judged by showing him a selection of threads and asking him to pick out particular hues. One of Belgrave's future squadron comrades sported a monocle but it didn't block his selection – or hinder his later ability to shoot down enemy aircraft for that matter.

It was surprising that the RFC was as well developed as it was. When it came to military aviation, Britain had lagged alarmingly behind the other European powers, and particularly France, before the war. The Wright Brothers had demonstrated powered flight at Kitty Hawk in 1903 and Louis Blériot's hop across the Channel six years later served notice that Britain could no longer count on its island status militarily. However, the top brass were woefully slow to catch on to the aeroplane's worth as a reconnaissance tool and more. In 1910 the Chief of the Imperial General Staff decried the notion of military flying as a useless and expensive fad and contemptuous cavalrymen, jealous of their role as the Army's eyes in battle, warned that aircraft would only frighten the horses. Luckily, there were enough enthusiastic pioneers of flying to demonstrate the value of their primitive contraptions and an Air Battalion of the Royal Engineers was formed on April 1 1911, charged with training men in the handling of kites, balloons and aeroplanes. It formed the nucleus of the Royal Flying Corps when that was established under Royal Warrant on April 13 1912 with the motto Per Ardua ad Astra – Through Adversity to the Stars. However, following mobilisation on August 4 1914 the mere four squadrons earmarked to accompany the British Expeditionary Force represented the entire operational strength of the fledgling force.

Fortunately Kitchener had the foresight to order a wholesale expansion but the problems, including an initial reliance on engines of French manufacture, were huge. There was much still to do by the time Belgrave joined the RFC on July 20 1916. His aviation career proper started on August 5 when he reported to No 2 School of Military Aeronautics in Oxford where some of the colleges had been taken over by the War Office. There he learned the theory of flight and how it was applied in the canvas, wood and wire aircraft of the day. The mysteries of aero engines – magnetos, carburettors and lubrication systems – were explained by technical experts. Map-reading, Morse, magnetism, meteorology and clock codes for specifying direction were all on the timetable for his month of head-spinning induction. Much of the instruction dealt with equipment already heading for obsolescence. It did nothing to prepare students for new developments. As a result the would-be fliers emerged with a basic knowledge suitable for the previous year not for the year they faced. Neither did the cramming sessions provide answers to the points Belgrave and his fellow tyros constantly pondered. What exactly was the sensation of flying like? Did they have the necessary nerve? Would they be able to function properly in the freezing, oxygen-starved environment two miles above the earth? Not that any doctor had seemed unduly concerned that Belgrave, having been gassed, might face breathing difficulties flying at such altitudes.

Some answers were to be provided soon enough for, on September 7, Belgrave was posted to the Central Flying School at Upavon in Wiltshire. It was there on Salisbury Plain that he made his first acquaintance with the Rumpety, the nickname for one of the RFC's principal training aircraft, the Maurice Farman S11. This machine, of comic appearance to modern eyes and even in 1916 too antiquated for its original service role, was usually dubbed the MF Shorthorn because of the short landing skids at the front. These distinguished it from the earlier MF7, which had an additional forward elevator on projecting booms and longer skids and was inevitably known as the Longhorn. The Shorthorn, of French origin, was a 'pusher' biplane with the engine and propeller behind the two-man crew to push the machine through the air. Student and instructor sat in tandem in a nacelle perched high at the front of the aircraft. There was no fuselage as such, merely a frame of tubes extending rearwards to where the tail was mounted. The wings were braced with criss-crossing external wires and more wiring linked the pilot's controls with the movable air surfaces, the whole system being known as the birdcage.

Belgrave and his contemporaries were kept in the dark about the Shorthorn's two chief design defects. The aircraft's centre spars were arched for extra strength to bear the weight of engine, fuel and crew during landings. Unfortunately there was a trade-off – a weakness when side loads were applied and this may have been the main factor in terrifying and sometimes lethal cases of wings breaking in flight. Also the cambered, lifting tailplane provided less fore-and-aft stability than a non-lifting stabiliser and lift from it could automatically increase the steepness of a dive and make it heart-stoppingly tricky for the pilot to pull up. Few instructors had sufficient knowledge of aerodynamics to analyse the defects and advise their pupils accordingly. They merely knew the Shorthorn was docile enough flying level when its top speed was about 60mph. It was easiest to tell new pilots to fly fairly sedately and avoid any manoeuvres that could remotely be termed stunting.

Calm air was needed for instruction. In high summer lessons were usually restricted to early morning or late evening to avoid the rising air pockets caused when the sun heated the ground. But that was not usually too much of a problem in September and suitable conditions for Belgrave's first flight were not long in coming. His flying logbook has not come to light so the exact date of his first venture into the air is not known. Doubtless his instructor demonstrated how to negotiate a way through the birdcage and use the footholds to climb into the nacelle. A carelessly placed foot could easily damage the frail structure. Belgrave lowered himself into the front seat where he was fully exposed to the elements. Sporting the ungainly leather crash helmet obligatory for all pupils, he must have felt a mixture of excited anticipation and sheepishness at being perched in full view of ground crew and novices awaiting their turn. The instructor took the seat behind him, a position occupied during active service by an observer armed with a Lewis gun. The nacelle's side panel, lowered to ease entry, was pulled up and bolted. Belgrave was then indoctrinated into the ritual necessary to persuade the engine to start. An ack emma (signallers' term for air mechanic) stood caged within the wires and tubes behind the propeller. This man first checked by question and answer that the pilot's ignition was switched off and fuel turned on. Then to prime the engine with fuel he turned the two-blade wooden propeller a few times by hand. The pilot, when he heard the cry of 'Contact, Sir', switched on the ignition and confirmed he had done so by calling back 'Contact'. At that stage the ack emma hopefully heaved the propeller a quarter turn while the pilot twirled the hand starter magneto to boost the spark at the plugs. With any luck the 70hp Renault rattled into life after one or two heaves and the ack emma could emerge from his cage.

The fuel tank, between the rear seat and the engine, was dangerously placed. In a crash the hot engine could break away from its mounting, rupture the tank and ignite its contents. The flaming mass might then fall on the aircrew. The commander of at least one pusher squadron ordered his fliers not to use safety belts, believing it better for them to be thrown clear in a crash rather than remain trapped in the blazing wreckage. It can be assumed that Belgrave pushed such thoughts out of his mind as he felt the instructor waggling the flying controls. A dual set was fitted for the student, who placed his hands lightly on the 'spectacles' on top of the vertical control column to get a feel of the necessary inputs. Rocking these spectacles operated the ailerons. Fore and aft movement of the column controlled the elevator. At this stage Belgrave was told to keep his feet clear of the pedals which operated the twin rudders. Soon the Shorthorn was pointing into what little wind there was and the racket of the engine rose as the instructor increased the power. The pistons of the air-cooled V8 slapped against the cylinder walls, valves and tappets chattered away. The propeller revolved on an extension of the camshaft at half-speed and the reduction gear added to the noise. Since the Renault could not be enclosed and had only a scoop to direct the air flow on to its cylinders there was nothing to deaden the racket. It was perhaps this medley of sounds as it accompanied the drumming of the propeller and the song of piano wires – rumpety, rumpety rump – that earned the Shorthorn its nickname.

A few bounds over the grass and Belgrave was airborne. He was probably surprised at how little sensation of speed he experienced once the Shorthorn was off the ground. It seemed to float along. His instructor demonstrated a gentle turn or two and after five minutes the aircraft was lined up for landing. With the engine phut-phutting at tickover speed, the instructor pushed down the nose, rounded out a few feet above the grass and with a few gentle bumps the Rumpety was safely back down.

More dual lessons followed. It was difficult in the air for the instructor to explain what he wanted his student to do. There wasn't even a speaking tube. If the instructor wanted to say something he had to throttle back the engine and shout. Belgrave was told to place his hands and feet on the controls while the instructor demonstrated climbing, flying level, gliding and correcting for air bumps. Particular attention was needed during take-offs and landings, when there was most potential for accidents. Soon Belgrave was allowed almost complete control while his instructor sat nervously poised to take over if things went awry. The instructor would press his hand on Belgrave's right or left shoulder to indicate which way he wanted him to turn. A push or pull on his helmet meant nose down or up. Between flights, Belgrave stood with other pupils awaiting their turn in the air and apprehensively discussing terrors such as the stall. This happened when an aircraft's speed was allowed to drop sufficiently for lift to be lost, causing the machine to fall out of control. Immediate and decisive control inputs were the only way to prevent a serious crash, always providing the aircraft was high enough. The risk of a stall was ever present with the Shorthorn. It had lots of drag and the range of its flying speed was only about 20mph so as soon as the engine power was throttled back it was vital to push down the nose before the aircraft slowed perilously to the point of stalling. Yet pupils were not shown a stall and its effects. If a pilot entered a stall later when flying solo he did so because of his own incompetence or a risky desire to experiment.

Within a couple of weeks Belgrave was ready to fly solo and a suitably calm day arrived. To him, like all novices, that first solo flight was an intensely lonely experience. Perched in his seat, aircraft lined up for take-off, engine running, Belgrave had an overwhelming feeling that for the first time his destiny was in his own hands and his alone. Fears of crashing or, nearly as bad, making a mess of things in front of his watching instructor and fellow pupils, had to be fought down as the Rumpety gathered speed. Belgrave was surprised at how readily his machine took to the air, unburdened by the instructor's weight. A climb to about 500ft and a few gingerly conducted turns to keep the airfield close and exhilaration started to triumph over apprehension. Belgrave could see the khaki-clad figures below as they appraised his performance. Doubtless ack emmas observing his manoeuvres were musing whether he would be presenting them with yet another repair job. After a few minutes it was time to land, the trickiest part of the exercise. He positioned the machine into wind and eased the nose forward as he decreased power, the threat of stalling uppermost in his mind. Belgrave succeeded in bringing the Rumpety back to earth safely. For a moment he could bask in the congratulations of his fellows, the first big hurdle of his flying career cleared in triumph.

Belgrave had only brief chances for relaxation during his stint at the Central Flying School. However, Norman Macmillan, who went solo about four months after him, told in *Into The Blue*, his wonderfully evocative book about Great War flying, how young officers would hope to cadge a car ride into Salisbury to escape the isolation of life on a military camp. The seventeen-mile drive along the Lower Avon valley for a meal at the Haunch of Venison and the chance to see a theatre show were favourite memories for Macmillan. He later served with No 45 Squadron at the same time as Belgrave.

As Belgrave completed his first weeks of flying, the names of a handful of outstanding aviators were beginning to be known by the public despite the authorities being huffy about headline-seeking. Belgrave and his comrades were anxious for the chance to emulate the likes of Albert Ball, who had already been victorious in up to thirty aerial combats. Ball, a mere six weeks older than Belgrave, had just moved to No 60 Squadron, where the younger man would eventually make his mark. Son of a mayor of Nottingham, Ball was a quiet and diminutive chap yet courageous, aggressive and utterly relentless when seeking prey during the lone patrols which were his speciality. The Germans were quicker than the British to realise the propaganda value of young, valiant and photogenic airmen. But it was a two-edged sword; German morale had taken a knock that June when Max Immelmann, the feted 'Eagle of Lille', fell. Meanwhile for Belgrave there was still much to do before he could realise his dream of flying in the company of aces (a term, often derided by the pilots themselves, for a man with five confirmed aerial victories) let alone becoming one himself. On September 26, the day before his 20th birthday, he was posted to No 55 Squadron for the next stage of flying instruction. It is difficult to pin down his exact movements at this stage as the records are sketchy. No 55 Squadron had been formed a few months earlier at Castle Bromwich to the east of Birmingham. As each new flight of the squadron was formed it was sent to Lilbourne airfield, near Rugby and about six miles from the Belgrave homelands at North Kilworth. However, it is doubtful whether Belgrave made that move for by October 27 he was with No 28 Reserve Squadron, having been appointed Flying Officer. His new squadron was also at Castle Bromwich. Both squadrons came under 25th Wing and, as No 55 Squadron was short of accommodation and aircraft, it may be that it was simply expedient to transfer him. Castle Bromwich aerodrome, famous as the base for manufacture and testing of Spitfires in the Second World War, was expanding rapidly in 1916 as training needs grew. It had started with a flying school when tents and the jockeys' quarters at the local race course were requisitioned. Old Hall farmhouse became the officers' mess and huts were erected. But by the time of Belgrave's arrival the aerodrome was a station for the formation of squadrons and their working-up to operational efficiency. (The aerodrome was closed in 1959 and the land is now given over to housing).

At Castle Bromwich Belgrave became familiar with the BE2, RE7 and Avro 504 aircraft. Unlike the Farman, these biplane trainers were of 'tractor' design, with the engine and propeller at the front. The BE2 – the initials stood for Blériot Experimental – was designed for the Government by Geoffrey de Havilland, who was to become a legendary name in aircraft production. It was the mainstay of the RFC when the first squadrons flew to France. The two-seater was slow, sedate and inadequately armed and by late 1915 Stability Jane, as its BE2c variant was dubbed, had become a death trap for pilots in the face of the 'Fokker Scourge'. In the constant struggle to develop superior machinery the Germans had attained temporary ascendancy with their Fokker Eindecker. This monoplane had the crucial advantage of a machine-gun synchronised to fire through the propeller arc, allowing its pilots to point the aircraft where they wanted to shoot. By Belgrave's time the BE2 was really only good for a training role and he flew several of its variants.

The RE7 and Avro 504 were also two-seaters. Flying the Avro gave Belgrave his first valuable experience of a machine with a rotary engine, which had pronounced effects on performance and handling. The Avro 504, a product of A V Roe's company, later of Lancaster bomber fame, was destined to be developed into the RAF's standard trainer. Finally Belgrave converted to the Sopwith $1\frac{1}{2}$-Strutter, the type he would be flying in France. No 28 Reserve Squadron had only one flight of these machines at the time Belgrave was there because they were in short supply. The $1\frac{1}{2}$-Strutter was so called because of its short centre-section struts. It was the first British machine to have a machine-gun, in this case a single, belt-fed Vickers, that fired through the propeller arc. The Strutter was originally sponsored by the Royal Naval Air Service but the RFC saw its potential as a counter to the Fokker Eindecker. In active service, the observer/gunner in the rear seat had a Lewis machine-gun mounted on a Scarff ring, which allowed it to be swivelled, raised and lowered in any direction with ease. The Lewis was fed by detachable drums of ammunition. By November 29, Belgrave's hurried training was over and, with less than three months' flying experience to his credit, he was thought ready to rejoin the war and was posted to No 45 Squadron. A fellow member of No 28 Reserve Squadron, 19-year-old 2nd Lt Edward Erlebach, from Birchington in Kent, was also sent to No 45 and the pair travelled overseas together. Belgrave, like many RFC fliers, retained his old regiment's uniform. Only the pilot's wings proudly displayed on his tunic were evidence of his new role.

Belgrave and his companion arrived at No 1 Aircraft Depot near St Omer on November 30. That same day they were driven the eight miles west to Boisdinghem where No 45 Squadron and its $1\frac{1}{2}$-Strutters were temporarily based. The squadron was about to be moved and the hustle of preparation left little time for making replacement pilots from England feel particularly welcome. To add to the reasonable nervousness of new boys, it was soon made clear to Belgrave and Erlebach that they would be sent back home without ceremony if their flying abilities did not pass muster. The squadron's Commanding Officer, Major Willie Read, was exasperated with the standard of some of the pilots being sent to him. He had already sent back three 'duds' to receive further training and was ready to wield the axe again even though higher authority was strongly against it. It is worth backtracking here to explain what lay behind the uncertain atmosphere which Belgrave could hardly fail to discern as he tried his best to settle in at No 45 Squadron and get the measure of his new CO.

Major William Ronald Read, MC, of the 1st (King's) Dragoon Guards, had much experience of both combat and instructional flying. He learned to fly in 1913 and first went to France with No 3 Squadron at the beginning of the war. He was wounded in November 1914 but after more service in France and

England he became No 45 Squadron's CO on April 24 1916 a few weeks after its formation at Gosport. By then in his late twenties, Willie Read exuded an air of pipe-smoking maturity beneath which lay a personality inclined to the headstrong and obstinate. When he took No 45 to France in mid-October he was furious to find that the accommodation at the squadron's bleak airfield at Fienvillers, six miles west-south-west of Doullens, was scandalously deficient. There was a lack of tents, and no blankets, rations or even water had been laid on for the squadron. Three other squadrons were already there, making the whole set-up very crowded. Read was also put out that Lieutenant Colonel H C T 'Stuffy' Dowding, commander of 9th Wing under which No 45 Squadron was to serve, was not there to greet it. The two men had previously rowed at the Central Flying School. At Fienvillers Read clashed with Dowding again by quartering his men in the hangars and leaving his squadron's twelve Sopwiths picketed outside. When Dowding – who, as Air Marshal Sir Hugh Dowding, was Fighter Command's chief in the Battle of Britain – did show up he ordered the men to be turfed out. More seriously, despite Read wanting time for his squadron to settle in, Dowding, or 'The Cherub' as Read referred to him in private, demanded lots of flying. This spelled disaster as the squadron's green pilots came up against crack German fliers. In its first week in France, which involved just three days of operations, the squadron had six men killed in action, a seventh badly wounded and two others injured in a flying accident. Dowding blamed the losses on inefficiency. Read was outraged.

The situation worsened until the squadron hit probably its lowest point on October 27 when its effective strength stood at seven pilots, thirteen observers and thirteen aircraft. On November 5 the squadron moved to Boisdinghem and was temporarily withdrawn from operations, allowing time for it to regain its balance. After ten days operational sorties restarted but these were largely defensive and no aircraft crossed the lines. Crucially, the missions gave crews much needed experience and a boost in confidence. This was the state of affairs when Belgrave arrived as one of twelve replacement officers to join No 45 during December. Among the newcomers were two Castle Bromwich graduates typical of the Empire's growing contribution to the RFC. Henry Fitchat, from South Africa, and Hubert Solomon, from New Zealand, were both second lieutenants who had been with No 54 Squadron.

Read's attitude to newcomers did not indicate lack of sympathy for those in his charge. On the contrary, the former cavalryman's concern for his men's welfare and his protests at what he perceived to be unreasonable demands placed on his squadron would continue to be a source of friction between him and his superiors even though No 45 Squadron was now assigned to 11th (Army) Wing, away from Dowding's direct scrutiny. Obviously Read recognised it was hardly the newcomers' fault that their preparation had been so lacking. Accepting that he could not return every pilot who had not reached the required standard, he instituted his own training programme so that men could be eased, rather than be thrust ill-prepared, into combat. Lessons, fitted around operational requirements, were introduced to rectify the deficiencies of pilots who had never been taught to fly in formation, spin an aircraft and recover, loop, roll or bank more than forty-five degrees. In particular, Read insisted on lots of circuit flying to practise the art of landing, crucial if the notoriously delicate undercarriages of the Strutters were to avoid damage from heavy or skewed arrivals back to earth. The problem of insufficient training was not unique to No 45 Squadron. Inexperienced pilots were committed to battle too soon because it was the only way to satisfy the demands of the RFC's expansion and make good the considerable losses being sustained through combat and accidents. Brigadier General David Henderson, first commander of the RFC in the field, had summed up the paradox earlier: 'The loss rate is high because training is short, but training is short because the loss rate is so high.'

For Belgrave, there was little time to take to the air before No 45 moved on December 4. Its new aerodrome was at Ste-Marie-Cappel in the flat Flanders farmlands about fifteen miles east of St Omer. From there it was to undertake the vital work of flying photo-reconnaissance and offensive patrols over the Ypres salient. The squadron's new patch, which included Ypres, Menin, Roulers and Courtrai, had a reputation as a 'hot corner'. Ypres itself had been recaptured from the Germans in October 1914 and the area to the east of the town would for four years be the scene of some of the harshest fighting of any war in history. It was in the skies above this pock-marked landscape of Belgium and northern France that Belgrave could look forward to taking his second crack at the enemy. Ste-Marie-Cappel was a little over twenty miles north-west from the spot where he had been knocked out of action with the infantry fifteen months before. He was quietly pleased when he saw the accommodation at the aerodrome and longer-serving pilots and observers confirmed that it was certainly a huge improvement on Fienvillers. The squadron had the aerodrome to itself. Officers' quarters and messes were in Nissen huts. These were not particularly spacious and were decidedly chilly as winter started to bite but Belgrave recognised it was all vastly preferable to the infantry dugouts that had been his home the previous year. There were good Bessonneau hangars, with girders covered by camouflaged canvas, and huts for repair shops. Because of the large amount of metal construction in the hangars it was thought wise to 'swing' the aircraft compasses, that is calculate any errors resulting from needles deviating from north because of the interference. In his superb history of No 45 Squadron, *The Flying Camels*, Wing Commander C G 'Jeff' Jefford relates how a captain from Wing arrived to deal with the compasses. He told one of the pilots his compass had been thirty degrees in error. 'Thank God I never use it!' came the response. The day after the squadron arrived at Ste-Marie-Cappel a gale threatened to destroy one of the hangars. Captain Eric Lubbock, commander of B Flight, who had been with the squadron from the outset, ordered some of the mechanics to climb up and secure the canvas. They were reluctant to risk their necks so Lubbock, in an act typical of his decisive and courageous nature, clambered into the rigging himself, inspiring enough of the men to follow him and prevent the structure collapsing.

Two old Maxim guns were provided to defend the aerodrome from aerial attack but they never brought anything down. The grass field itself was only about four hundred yards square. At the south-east corner a narrow strip of grass extended the east-west run by fifty yards. Two roads bordered the flying ground and there were road and field ditches over a yard deep and wide. A hedge partly obscured the hangars. At the south-west corner high poplar trees surrounded a farmstead which was out of bounds to all ranks. In brief, the aerodrome had traps galore for inexperienced or unwary pilots regardless of the direction from which they approached to land. In line with Read's policies for newcomers, Belgrave was first taken up in the observer's cockpit of a Strutter for a couple of trips so that an experienced pilot could familiarise him with local landmarks. Belgrave soon saw that Ste-Marie-Cappel was well blessed with 'signposts' for a pilot returning from a sortie. On one hill less than two miles north-east of the airfield was the little Flemish town of Cassel. Just south of the hill, at Oxelaere, was the headquarters of 2nd Brigade RFC, under which No 45 served via 11th Wing. To the east of Cassel rose the forested Mont des Recollets. These two hills formed natural beacons on which pilots could home visually. Belgrave noted other helpful features: the good roads leading to Ste-Marie-Cappel from Poperinghe and Ypres and from Bailleul and Armentières, the railway between Dunkirk and

Béthune, the lakes, such as tadpole-shaped Dickebusch and triangular Zillebeke, the forests and the strategically placed sausage balloons. There was also the black scar of the front line. And as Belgrave was to learn, the Channel and Dover's white cliffs were tantalisingly visible from altitude on a clear day.

On his familiarisation trips Belgrave could see the back of the pilot's helmeted head four feet in front of him. The pilot glanced at him occasionally through a small round mirror mounted on steel supports beneath the upper wing. The pair could also communicate through the speaking tube, a length of rubber piping which passed through the fuselage. There were no dual controls, however, so on their return to the airfield, Belgrave took care to notice the angle and speed of approach, ever mindful of the Strutter's alarming tendency to continue floating just above the ground before touchdown. A small field like Ste-Marie-Cappel could catch out even expert fliers. On December 6 the squadron flew its first operation over the Ypres front under the auspices of 11th Wing, which had its headquarters at Bailleul. Three patrols were flown, without loss, although two aircraft developed technical problems and had to land at Abeele. The weather was starting to hamper flying and the squadron was sometimes grounded by fog. The first snow fell on December 12. That did not prevent Belgrave from gaining flying practice next day which, if nothing else, confirmed to him the fickle nature of the 110hp Clergêt engines with which the squadron's Strutters were fitted.

That morning he took up Struuter A1071 for a twelve-minute solo practice flight, which was uneventful. He encountered a thin layer of cloud at low level though it was quite clear above 1,000ft. At noon he joined other pilots to practise formation flying. His observer was 22-year-old Lt Francis Truscott, who had joined the squadron seven weeks before, having previously served in the Suffolk Regiment. His father Sir George Wyatt Truscott, the first baronet, had been Lord Mayor of London in 1908 and was a staunch Freemason and governor of several hospitals in the capital. Belgrave and Truscott had been airborne barely five minutes when an oily distributor on Sopwith 7789 robbed the engine of power and they were forced to land a mile west of the airfield. Mechanics were dispatched to rectify the problem and a little over an hour later Belgrave flew the machine back to Ste-Marie-Cappel alone, Truscott having scrounged a ride with the ground crew. The engine was still running roughly but Belgrave, ever conscious that he was still on probation, could at least congratulate himself on not having bent the aircraft in the unscheduled landing. He took up A7780 that afternoon for a further thirty minutes of practice. Belgrave used the same aircraft for a seventeen-minute flight next morning, hardly intensive training but a worthwhile increment to his stock of experience nevertheless.

Then on the morning of December 15 he teamed up for the first time with Sub Lt John Thompson, formerly of the Royal Naval Volunteer Reserve. Thompson, who had been with No 45 since late October, was destined to partner Belgrave as observer in some hair-raising exploits but on their first outing they contented themselves with eighteen minutes of routine practice. Belgrave was joined by Truscott that afternoon in A1071 for a slightly longer trip. All this activity was monitored by the ack emmas, who were kept busy straightening out the inadequate undercarriages of clumsily landed Strutters. The resourceful ground crews managed to cut their workload a little by pushing wooden broom handles into the axles to strengthen them.

On December 16 Belgrave and Thompson took off for some real work at last. They completed a successful fifty-minute reconnaissance flight in A1071 though they kept well back from the Front because at that stage the squadron had yet to be cleared to fly over German-held territory – perhaps HQ RFC had learned the folly of committing inexperienced units to unrestricted operations before they had time to acclimatise sufficiently. The pair rounded off the day practising formation flying under the leadership of Captain Lubbock. They were joined by Erlebach, Fitchat and 2nd Lt John Marshall, a pilot who had arrived from No 28 Reserve Squadron a week before. Marshall, only 19 and from Huntingdonshire, had started his war in a Cyclists' Battalion. Four new Strutters had been delivered to Ste-Marie-Cappel that day, raising the squadron's establishment of aircraft to its allotted eighteen. However, there were still only sixteen pilots and twelve observers available to fly them, though the continuing influx of newcomers would rectify that. Despite Read's dismay at the standard of some of the latest intakes none was sent home and it slowly dawned on Belgrave and his fellow tyros that No 45 would be their home for a little while yet. Belgrave and Thompson joined other crews for formation flying and to test their guns on December 17. They headed west towards the sea but had to turn back when near Boulogne as clouds closed in. When Belgrave touched down that afternoon he had been in the air for 1hr 25mins, his longest flight from Ste-Marie-Cappel to date and that without engine trouble. However, engine problems were a constant source of complaint and two days later Belgrave took A1071 for a forty-minute test flight without discovering why its engine failed to rev properly on the ground but performed satisfactorily in the air. The squadron flew a particularly useful reconnaissance mission that day and on December 20 Belgrave and Thompson were among nine crews involved in two more successful reconnaissances. There was no praise forthcoming from Wing HQ, though, noted an aggrieved Read.

On December 22 Belgrave and Thompson took up A1071 for more than an hour of formation flying practice. There was no operational flying the following day. However, Willie Read put Corporal Robert Fleming in the back of a Strutter and, with two other crews, risked rising winds to make the brief hop to St Omer. There some of the pilots were lucky enough to try out a triplane, Sopwith Pup and Nieuport scout, nimble single-seaters that came as a revelation after their somewhat pedestrian Strutters. Later that day plans for the squadron's Christmas celebrations took a knock when gales demolished some of the smaller hangars. One of these was used as the men's mess and a stage had already been erected in it for the squadron party. As Christmas approached, Belgrave looked back on nearly four weeks with the squadron. He was satisfied that his flying had improved immeasurably, he felt at home in the Strutters and had learned the importance of a good rapport with the observers. However, he would not feel a fully-fledged member of No 45 Squadron until he had met the foe in the air. The opportunity would not be long in coming.

# CHAPTER FOUR

# AN ACE

CHRISTMAS Eve. Yet there was no question of James Belgrave and his comrades demonstrating any goodwill to the Germans who were looking forward to their own *Frohe Weihnachten* on the other side of the lines some twenty miles to the east. On the bleak morning of December 24 1916 Belgrave tugged on his sheepskin flying boots, leather coat, great gauntlets and fur-lined flying cap and trudged out to Strutter A1071, one of four Sopwiths primed and ready for a defensive patrol by B Flight. The term defensive patrol would come to mean a probe up to five miles behind German positions but the orders that day were to fly directly above the trenches and no further – what would later be called a line patrol. The squadron was still barred from crossing the Front. Belgrave lowered himself into the Sopwith's wicker seat and checked the ammunition feed to the Vickers mounted in front of him. His observer, John Thompson, busied himself in the rear cockpit, ensuring the free movement of his Lewis gun on its mounting and checking that the spare ammunition drums, Very pistol, flares and his revolver were securely stowed.

The same routine was being followed in the other aircraft. In A1064 Captain Lubbock, commanding the flight, was paired with his regular and well-trusted observer, 2nd Lt Frank Austin. Lt Cecil Griffin, one of the pilots who had flown the squadron's first aircraft to France, was at the controls of A1072 with 2nd Lt Denys Greenhow in the rear cockpit. Greenhow was the son of a clergyman from

Eastbourne, Sussex, and had been educated at Lancing College. Marshall, in 7800, had Truscott as his observer. A little after 10am it was time to start the engines. The procedure was much the same as for the Farman but, because the Strutter had its engine at the front, the ack emma swinging the propeller took particular care with his footing so that he did not find himself in the path of the rotating blades should the aircraft lurch forward on starting. With the engine running, Belgrave monitored the oil pulsing through an inspection glass. After a minute's warm-up he opened the throttle to test the engine while chocks in front of each wheel restrained the machine. An ack emma stood at each wing-tip and a third caught the full blast of the slipstream as he draped his body over the tail-end of the fuselage to prevent the Strutter tipping on its nose, letting the prop strike the ground. Satisfied that the engine was performing properly, Belgrave throttled back and waved a hand side to side above his head, signalling for the chocks to be removed by a tug on their ropes and for the man at the rear to get off. With his safety belt tightened and goggles adjusted, Belgrave taxied out behind the other machines.

At about 10.15am he was airborne and after circling the airfield to gain height he and the other pilots set course eastwards towards the lines. Grateful for his recent practice in keeping station in the air, Belgrave held his place in the flight's V formation. When he glanced from behind the Sopwith's tiny windshield the blast of icy air cut through leather and fur. For Thompson it was much worse. The observer lived in a constant hurricane as he turned and twisted on the lookout for German machines. About forty minutes into the patrol it was Lubbock, with his keen and experienced eyes, who first spotted an enemy aeroplane over Steenwerke. He fired a red flare to alert his comrades and opened fire on the large Aviatik. The range was too great and his guns jammed repeatedly. Austin also tried a few shots but the German flew off towards Lille and safety. It was not long before Lubbock spotted another potential prey at 13,000ft above Bailleul. This time it was an Albatros and Lubbock tried to cut off the German's line of retreat. However, the enemy proved far too fast to catch as he dived eastwards, crossing the lines at 6,000ft. With the patrol still near Bailleul, a two-seater Halberstadt flying towards Ypres soon presented itself as a third target. Lubbock pushed down the nose of his Strutter to overtake the German, allowing Austin to fire half a drum. The Halberstadt went into a shallow dive but Lubbock pushed the Strutter until he was doing 130mph – this in an aircraft which normally trundled along at 80mph when above 10,000ft.

Marshall dived to give Lubbock support and his observer, Truscott, opened fire. Marshall then tried to get in position to use his front gun but was prevented from firing by a British machine, an FE2b, which appeared from nowhere and baulked him. With great skill Lubbock manoeuvred his Strutter to a position twenty yards from the enemy machine and almost directly under it. This allowed Austin to fire continuously while the Halberstadt was unable to bring either of its guns to bear. The German pilot did his best to shake off the Strutter by zig-zagging for ten miles as he flew towards Roulers but Lubbock could not be budged. By the time the aircraft were over Roulers at 5,500ft Austin had emptied two full drums of ammunition and it was time to break off the combat. Of three hundred rounds fired at the German machine, about half had hit home, many appearing to enter the fuselage just behind the pilot's seat. Despite being thus riddled, the Halberstadt refused to fall, proving just how much damage the aircraft of the period could survive as long as bullets did not hit vital engine components, flying controls or the pilot.

Griffin had also dived on one of the German machines and managed to fire forty rounds before being forced to flatten out as his Strutter's speed built to perilous levels. A little later he spotted tell-tale puffs of anti-aircraft fire, nicknamed 'Archie', exploding in the sky west of Ypres. They were white, indicating a German aircraft was the target – enemy Archie was black. He saw the machine, which had a white band round the fuselage, at 14,000ft and climbed to engage it. The German aeroplane, an Aviatik, turned west then almost immediately east. Griffin fired about three hundred rounds. His observer Greenhow emptied one double drum into the top wings of the German. Many tracers were seen to strike home but the aeroplane seemed under perfect control when the British pair last saw it diving towards Courtrai.

Belgrave was determined not to be left out of the action. At 10,000ft to the north-east of Ypres he spotted a German machine, white with black stripes either side of the black crosses on its wings, and dived to the attack. It was not to be Belgrave's day for a victory, however. The enemy pilot was flying south-west but, on seeing the British formation, he dived towards the south-east. Belgrave gave chase and opened fire but the German, already at a considerable distance, opened the gap as he picked up speed in the dive. Then Belgrave's engine became choked and would fire only intermittently between splutters. Finally it cut out altogether, leaving Belgrave with no choice but to glide westwards. He succeeded in putting the Strutter down safely at No 42 Squadron's aerodrome at

Bailleul. Lubbock, meanwhile, found the German anti-aircraft guns very active on his way home. Amid the characteristic 'woof woof' sound of Archie, his Strutter was rocked by shells breaking above his right wing. Lubbock could smell the cordite and hear the deadly hiss of shrapnel. After landing at Ste-Marie-Cappel he found the wing surface had been pierced by metal fragments and his lower wing and patrol leader's streamer had each been holed by machine-gun bullets. Marshall, who had caught up with Lubbock on the way home, and Griffin, who had failed to rejoin his comrades after all the excitement, both got back safely. The patrol was the squadron's first direct engagement with the enemy since the disastrous encounters of the previous October. Although no German had been downed, No 45 Squadron had certainly come out best and Lubbock rated it a 'topping fight'. His fliers were even back in time for lunch – minus Belgrave. He had to hang around at Bailleul until mechanics fettled his engine so that he could make the ten-minute hop back to Ste-Marie-Cappel, landing at 2.20pm. When he penned his first combat report later that day he added at the bottom a rough sketch of the HA that got away. (The use of HA as an abbreviation in combat reports for hostile aircraft was later discouraged by the authorities as it was widely thought to stand for Hun aircraft. The initials were superseded by EA, for enemy aircraft). Although his first clash with the enemy in the air had hardly been a glorious success, Belgrave was entitled to feel some muted satisfaction; he had done his best, proved not to be lacking in courage and had returned unscathed and fully ready for another go.

As he mused on the day's events Belgrave recognised that, in Lubbock, he already had the best possible teacher when it came to air fighting. Lubbock, the squadron's most determined and aggressive yet modest warrior, was always hungry for action. As Read noted in his diary after B Flight's Christmas Eve exploits: 'Lubbock shows himself a tiger for Hun chasing.' The CO's opinion of Lubbock was not consistently high, though. The two had had their differences of opinion and earlier in December Read, commenting in his journal about the perceived failings of all his flight commanders, wrote: 'I think Lubbock is about as incompetent as any of them. No control over his flight officers or men. He may improve as he is very young.' Jeff Jefford, chronicler of No 45 Squadron, suggests the friction between the two was all to do with their different styles. Read, the professional soldier and pre-war cavalryman used to issuing peremptory commands, perhaps initially assumed that Lubbock, a civilian in uniform for the duration, was failing to get things done because he did not hear him barking out orders. In fact, Lubbock was a natural leader and fine organiser, as respected as he was liked by the officers and men under his command.

The Hon Eric Fox Pitt Lubbock, born in 1893, was the son of Sir John Lubbock, who took the title Lord Avebury when he became the 1st Baron in 1900. The family's main home was a country house in Kent and there were other country properties and two town-houses in fashionable London streets. A glimpse of an aeroplane when Eric was 16 triggered a longing to fly. After Eton, he went up to Oxford in 1912 to read biology at Balliol. But war cut short Eric's university career and in September 1914 he enlisted as a private soldier in the Army Service Corps. He was sent to France where a chance meeting with an old friend serving as an RFC observer reawakened Eric's earlier interest in aviation. He decided to apply to be an officer in the RFC, which first involved gaining a readily granted commission in the ASC. While flying as an observer with No 5 Squadron in October 1915 he and his pilot shot down an Albatros, earning them both the Military Cross. It is no denigration of their gallantry to point out that at that stage of the war air-to-air combat was still in its infancy and the confirmed destruction of an enemy aircraft something of a novelty. Later it would be unusual for a decoration to be awarded on the basis of a single successful attack. Eric gained his pilot's wings in the summer of 1916 and was in at the formation of No 45 Squadron. He piloted one of the first five of the squadron's aircraft to land in France on October 14 that year and flew on its first operational mission six days later. As has been noted, that was the start of a bloody time for No 45.

For one day, however, the grim memories could be put aside. No operations were scheduled for December 25. The wind-battered hangars had been repaired and Christmas was celebrated in fine style. Two newly acquired pianos, one bought, one rented, helped the party along and there were ample supplies of booze. One of the riggers, Sergeant G Smith, was already the worse for wear by 10am and bet everyone he could climb the windsock mast and sit on it. He sat contentedly smoking on his chilly perch until talked down by Sergeant Major G Baker. Following seasonal tradition, Belgrave and the other officers and NCOs served the men their Christmas dinner. Squadron wags displayed a touch of public schoolboy humour by producing a menu listing specialities such as Cocktail Quarante Cinq, Rissoles de Poisson Inconnu, Sauce Hotair d'Escadron, Pommes de Terre Conrod and Choux de Bruxelles Sideslip to be followed by Pouding de Noel and Sauce Eau de Vie, washed down with Perrier Jouet 1066. The actual meal of turkey, ham, beef, potatoes and cabbage, Christmas pudding, pineapple and custard, was well received. As Read was raising his glass Baker, carrying a large dixie of spuds, tripped and spilled the lot at the CO's feet, adding to the merriment. After tea the NCOs and men staged a concert party. On Boxing Day the squadron received a visit from Lieutenant Colonel F W Richey, Officer Commanding 11th Wing, who had anything but seasonal greetings on his mind. B Flight had plainly crossed the Front in defiance of orders while pursuing the enemy two days previously and Richey was furious. In Willie Read's words, the Colonel 'came out with a fearful straff about my fellows going over the line'. Read was forced to pass on the warning to Lubbock that any repeat infringement would result in him being sent home in disgrace. Privately he was outraged by Richey's tirade and quietly advised Lubbock to take no notice. Lubbock dubbed the Colonel 'President of the Society for the Prevention of Cruelty to Huns' and vented his frustration by composing a piece of verse starting:

> A real good bit of straffing fun
> Was when we tried to straff the Hun,
> But funnier than anything
> Was the straffing we got from the Wing.
> 'We'll send you home', they said to me,
> 'If you attack the enemy'.

It was clearly insubordination but Read proved where his sympathies lay by merely copying the verses into his diary. Belgrave was too junior to get caught in the Boxing Day blast and in any case was off practising formation flying for fifty-five minutes in A1071 with Truscott in the back seat. He put in two more hours of practice the following day and two shorter sessions on December 28.

On December 29 Belgrave, or at least his observer Truscott, had the chance of another pop at the enemy. They were at 9,000ft between Ypres and Vlamertinge and preparing to take reconnaissance photographs when Truscott spotted a large German aircraft, probably an Aviatik, directly above them. Belgrave described in his combat report what happened next: 'The observer opened fire, and at the same time an FE2d close to us opened fire. The HA who had been proceeding west then turned north and then made south-east. We followed him over the trenches but were unable to climb up to him. He was apparently driven over his lines by our fire.' The following day Lieutenant Colonel G B Stopford took over as OC 11th Wing and Read would find that he would work at least a little better with him than he had done with Richey. The squadron was also getting into shape and was cleared to cross the lines – although not for another week, the delay being demanded perhaps as penance for Lubbock's infringement. Low clouds and strong winds ruled out much activity on New Year's Day 1917 although Belgrave was able to take up A1071 for a satisfactory engine test. Until the ban on crossing the lines was finally lifted Read was anxious to make the most of any spare time to press ahead with his training programme. His stress on thorough preparation for pilots would be vindicated eventually by RFC statistics. It would become clear that if sound training helped a pilot survive his first month of operations he had a reasonable chance of becoming competent, even successful, and then, with luck, he might even complete a tour of combat duty.

On January 2 Read was gratified that the squadron was able to cram in a full day of useful flying. The sorties included practice formation flying, two four-aircraft reconnaissances – keeping strictly to the friendly side of the lines, of course – plus gunnery and photography trips. Belgrave took part in one practice formation flight with Truscott in A1071. That afternoon air gunner Cpl R C Jenkins joined Belgrave in the same aircraft for a two-hour practice reconnaissance and photography sortie safely out of harm's way to the west, following the route Aire to St Pol to Etaples. Belgrave had no flying to do on January 3 apart from taking up A1071 to test its ever troublesome engine, which at least behaved itself the following day when he and Thompson were paired for a practice formation sortie. The gremlins struck again on January 4 when Belgrave, with Thompson, had to drop out of an eight-aircraft defensive patrol to make a forced landing, damaging the undercarriage. It came as no great surprise to ground crew who were still having to replace or straighten Strutters' axles at the rate of one or two a day. All seemed well with A1071 when Belgrave took up the aircraft for a test flight after repairs. The squadron flew whenever possible that month, usually on missions involving two or three though sometimes up to eight aircraft. However, clouds, rain and snow prevented or curtailed some patrols and there were only infrequent contacts with the enemy, usually inconclusive. Belgrave and Thompson joined a defensive patrol on January 15 but the operation was scrubbed after forty-five minutes when lowering cloud sent them back to Ste-Marie-Cappel. The continuing poor weather meant it was another five days before Belgrave could even start to fit in more practice sessions in A1071. Things started to hot up on January 22, however, when Belgrave, with Greenhow as observer, returned from patrol with five holes in the fabric of A1071 after running into Archie.

On Tuesday January 23 the squadron had its first major engagement with the enemy for three months, although Belgrave and Greenhow, this time in A1072, played only a minor role in the events of an extremely busy day. Two Strutters were first in the air at 7.30am. Belgrave and Greenhow, paired with another Strutter for a defensive patrol, followed, taking off at 10am. They spotted a German near Menin but he was too far away for them to engage him. Another three enemy aircraft were seen even further away. Belgrave thought it useful to report he had seen trains on the move out of Lille in enemy territory. He landed back at Ste-Marie-Cappel at 12.10pm. A formation of four more Strutters had already taken off and Belgrave was just in time to see another pair take to the sky. A further pair and another four-aircraft formation would be committed before darkness called a halt to operations. The two four-aircraft missions were the squadron's first attempts at using an oblique camera for photo-reconnaissance, although both were unsuccessful due to the weather. Before the end of the day Captain Bransby Williams and 2nd Lt Joseph Senior in A1083 claimed one enemy aircraft out of control and one damaged while the gunner in Lt Eric Hamilton's 7774, Air Mechanic 1st Class Frederick Lambert, claimed to have damaged another. The modest success came at a price. 2nd Lt Frank Courtney's observer in 7792, 2nd Lt Thomas Northcote, a New Zealander, was wounded. On one mission 2nd Lt James Lyle and Bombardier Alfred Harrison in A1078 had dropped out of formation, perhaps with engine trouble. The vulnerable Strutter was last seen over Dadizeele and was shot down by Leutnant Walter von Bülow-Bothkamp, of Jasta (short for Jagdstaffel or hunting squadron) 18, based at Halluin. It was the German's fifth victory. Lyle, aged 22, from Vernon, Lanarkshire, and Harrison, a Surrey man who had been in the Royal Horse Artillery, were later reported dead.

The following day Belgrave, in A1071 as usual, helped provide an escort for a photo-reconnaissance flight by No 42 Squadron. He spotted a German aircraft north-west of Lille but it was too far off to be engaged. Later he and Greenhow were on a two-hour defensive patrol over the trenches when Belgrave tested his Vickers only to find it jammed repeatedly. A mission on January 25 to escort another aircraft planning to take photographs over Becelaere to Courtrai turned to farce. Belgrave and Greenhow were recalled after five minutes because the camera was not working. They took off five minutes later only to be recalled when the camera malfunctioned again. They called it a day after they made a third start and the camera still failed to function.

On January 26, only three days after the loss of Lyle and Harrison, death struck the squadron again. But because of yet more trouble with unreliable A1071, Belgrave was not there to see the tragedy played out. Belgrave, with Corporal Jenkins, took off with four other Strutters for a photo-reconnaissance mission over Courtrai, Menin and Halluin. Captain Lawrence McArthur was leading the flight in A1076 with 2nd Lt Claude Emery as observer. They, along with Williams and Senior in A1075, were to take the photographs. Belgrave and Jenkins were acting as escort along with 2nd Lt Colin Campbell, a 33-year-old Canadian piloting A2381 with 2nd Lt John Vessey as observer, and Flt Sgt Walter Webb and Corporal Fleming in A1074. After fifty minutes and without having crossed the lines, Belgrave was forced to leave the formation with engine trouble and limp to Bailleul. The remaining aircraft flew east in V formation. With the photographing under way the Strutters were attacked and another victim was claimed by von Bülow-Bothkamp, who shot down Webb's aircraft in flames over Halluin. Almost at once the Strutter's tailplane fell away and the wreckage plunged to earth. The crew had no chance. The loss of Webb was particularly sad. He was virtually a founder member of the RFC, having transferred to the fledgling service from the Royal Engineers back in 1912, as his low service number 191 testified. He went to France as a mechanic but gained his wings in September 1915. Robert Fleming, from a farm family in Lanarkshire, was a craftsman who had volunteered for aerial gunner in November 1916. On the day of his death three other tradesmen were returned to their previous roles after failing to qualify for flying duties. Perhaps they were grateful, in view of Fleming's fate. Whether the repeated failures of A1071's Clergêt were in part down to Belgrave's clumsy engine management or merely par for the course for a hard-worked rotary is impossible to tell. All of No 45 Squadron's Strutters were prone to be left misfiring by troubles such as broken valve springs or rockers, damaged ignition leads and defective oil pumps, magnetos and spark plugs. More seriously, pistons could break or a cylinder could even blow off, damaging other parts of the aircraft. It was not unusual for mechanics to work all night changing an engine.

At about this time Willie Read was given more cause for exasperation. An order came through prohibiting squadron commanders from flying over the lines. The thinking was that any officer with sufficient experience and skill to become a Major was too valuable to risk losing. For men like Read, who believed a squadron should be led from the front, it was at best a frustration. Meanwhile the squadron was playing its full part in RFC operations. Its photo-reconnaissance work was vital. Squadrons such as No 45, serving under Army Wings, also attempted to provide co-ordinated cover for the Corps Wings engaged in artillery and infantry co-operation flights. Another task was to destroy or at least harry German reconnaissance machines. The whole RFC ethos was one of taking the war to the enemy whenever possible; an offensive patrol might venture twelve miles behind the German positions. As a result most aerial combats occurred on the enemy side of the lines and British aircraft which were shot down or suffered crippling damage or technical faults would usually fall in German-held territory. It was something of an achievement to make it home in a machine with ripped fabric, smashed timber and perhaps tanks holed by shell and bullet, forcing a pilot to rely on his emergency gravity tank.

A particularly violent encounter for No 45 Squadron, on February 7, gave Belgrave his first victory and found him helping to help extricate Lubbock from a perilous situation into the bargain. Belgrave was with Thompson in 7775, one of four Strutters escorting Lubbock's A1084 on a photo-reconnaissance flight. Lubbock's observer Austin had just exposed the first plate over Tourcoing at 10,000ft when four German single-seaters pounced on the British formation at 12.35pm. The extremely fast and manoeuvrable enemy scouts, painted green on top and yellow beneath, picked off the Strutter to the left and rear of Lubbock. It was 7789, piloted by Erlebach with Air Mechanic 2nd Class Frederick Ridgway as his gunner/observer. Thompson fired at one of the German machines as it swooped and Belgrave shot at another as it flashed past and dived away in front of him. It was too late. Erlebach's machine fell out of control and the wings folded up. The doomed aeroplane took an awful two minutes to reach the ground. Erlebach was killed but, astonishingly, Ridgway survived the impact though he died later that day. Lubbock, meanwhile, went on the attack with typical aggression. He became embroiled in six combats with four Germans in rapid succession though, as he stated later, 'it is hard to say where one fight ended and the next began'. His Vickers jammed after the third combat.

After five minutes of respite the fighting flared again further north over Menin, this time with only three Strutters involved because Henry Fitchat, with 2nd Lt W G Scotcher as observer, had retired to the safety of the British side of the lines with engine trouble. Belgrave, seeing an enemy aircraft above him, climbed and opened fire at fifty yards. The German machine, an Albatros, turned away and dived towards Courtrai with Belgrave in pursuit and still firing. Suddenly the enemy aircraft side-slipped then went into a vertical dive, out of control. Belgrave could not watch to see if it crashed because he saw Lubbock jousting with another German scout, both machines circling in an anti-clockwise direction in a desperate attempt to get into a firing position. The German turned his attention to Belgrave as he closed in and for a moment the two were flying parallel to one another with Belgrave slightly above. Belgrave's Vickers was out of ammunition and Thompson was temporarily unable to fire because the Strutter's bottom wing restricted his view. Belgrave soon manoeuvred into a position which allowed Thompson to empty a drum of Lewis ammunition into the German aircraft at very close range. The German dived away though apparently still under control. Captain John Mackay, in the remaining Strutter, 7800, also seems to have been victorious. Mackay, a Canadian who joined the squadron three weeks after Belgrave, had been at the right rear of the formation when Erlebach went down. Over Menin one of the Germans circled menacingly. Mackay's gun had jammed but his observer Truscott kept the enemy at bay by emptying a drum at him from two hundred yards. A second German then positioned himself behind and above the British crew and stalked them for six minutes. Truscott kept his nerve and held his fire until the German put his nose down to close the gap. At sixty yards Truscott started shooting and the German ceased firing at once. The enemy machine turned steeply to the left before plunging, apparently out of control, into Menin. Truscott fired at another machine with no apparent result. When the sky cleared of enemy aircraft the Strutters turned for home. Belgrave's satisfaction with his own performance was tempered by sadness at the loss of young Erlebach a little over two months after they had joined the squadron together. Erlebach's Strutter was the third and last of No 45's Strutters to fall to von Bülow-Bothkamp. The German would raise his tally of victories to twenty-eight before he was shot down and killed near Ypres on January 6 1918.

Next day Belgrave took up A1071 for a twenty-minute test after yet more work had been completed on its engine. All seemed well but predictably the engine then gave trouble when Belgrave and Thompson went up later in the day to escort Lubbock and Austin on another photographic mission. Belgrave and Thompson swapped to 7780 for a similar mission on February 9. This aircraft behaved impeccably, which was just as well because Belgrave again had to go to Lubbock's rescue in dramatic circumstances. The two Strutters were climbing towards the lines when Lubbock, in A1084, spotted British anti-aircraft shells bursting over Hazebrouck at about 12,000ft. He and Belgrave, still at about 8,000ft, climbed as quickly as they could but were over Béthune some fourteen miles to the south-east before they closed on the gunners' target, a German two-seater. Both pilots dived to the attack. Lubbock fired a hundred rounds before his gun jammed then turned to allow Austin to fire a drum. Belgrave swooped on the enemy aeroplane, which dived to 1,000ft before landing near Lille. This distraction had taken the British crews well south of their patrol area between Ypres and Houthulst Forest but they got back on track and Austin started taking his photographs. The work was again interrupted, this time by the sight of five aircraft approaching from the east. As no German guns were firing at them, Lubbock and Belgrave assumed they were hostile and, not liking the odds, headed closer to the lines. When they recognised the five as FE2bs they turned back eastwards to complete their photography.

Then the real excitement started. Two German scouts appeared from the direction of Roulers, flew over the forest and turned when a hundred yards from the Strutters and about a hundred feet above. Belgrave decided to take on the nearer one and opened fire with his front gun. The German immediately dived eastwards. Belgrave followed for a short distance then turned back to continue escorting Lubbock. It was a good thing he did because the second German had dived on Lubbock's tail and Austin's gun had jammed at the crucial moment. Lubbock flung A1084 violently right and left to throw off his opponent but the German was a skilled pilot and followed every move. Defenceless and foiled in his attempts to bring his front gun to bear, Lubbock resorted to looping the Strutter and managed to get in four shots at his attacker as he did so. When he flattened out at the end of the loop, though, the wily German again manoeuvred his nimble single-seater behind the Sopwith's tail. Lubbock zoomed for a second loop while Austin calmly continued his attempts to clear the jam in his Lewis. In the second loop one half of the Sopwith's tail folded back. The damage to the control surfaces made the aircraft extremely difficult to control and the Strutter went into a steep dive with the German still only feet away. Belgrave arrived in time to follow the two down. They were so close to each other that Belgrave could fire only two short bursts at the German for fear of hitting the Sopwith. When they got down to 5,000ft Austin finally freed his gun and fired a drum into the pursuer. The German turned east and dived towards Houthulst Forest. Belgrave followed, firing frequent bursts, until he was only 2,000ft above the trees. The German, apparently having suffered little or no damage, was widening the gap so Belgrave climbed away and returned towards to the lines. Lubbock, in a fine display of piloting skill, had eased his crippled machine out of its dive and nursed it back to friendly territory. He made a forced landing at Chateau Louvie, a couple of miles north of Poperinghe, after a flight lasting an exhausting 2hr 25mins. Lubbock climbed unscathed from A1084, which was too badly damaged for him to fly again. Austin had exposed thirty-six plates so they had achieved the aim of their mission. Lubbock happily acknowledged that, but for Belgrave's intervention, he would have been shot down.

There was more photographic reconnaissance work on February 13 when Belgrave, with Thompson, and Lubbock, with Austin, went up to expose a highly creditable fifty-two plates of the railway between Ypres and Roulers. The two pairs were airborne again next day with two more crews, when twenty-three plates were exposed. The effort and risk were for nothing. Oil on the camera lens meant the job was botched.

Later in the month Lubbock, with Belgrave as an ally, was at loggerheads with Willie Read over what both pilots considered a slur on B Flight's performance. The exact cause of the offending allegations is not clear but pride seems to have been pricked by the 'flippant attitude' of remarks in a return made about the squadron's aircraft and those of the Germans which had been brought down. Read noted in his diary: 'Lubbock came to me in a very insubordinate way about it…Lubbock is a stout pilot and works hard but has no idea of running a flight.' Belgrave and Mackay put in applications to be transferred to another squadron, such was their indignation. The following day, Monday February 19, Read 'had a general straff' at Lubbock, Belgrave and Mackay. On the Tuesday Belgrave pressed home his point with Read by asking for his transfer request to be forwarded to Wing HQ. That evening Read went to see Colonel Stopford about the affair and showed him Belgrave's application. 'He is coming out to see the children in the morning,' Read wrote. 'Belgrave, I think, is nursing a grievance.' Stopford arrived at Ste-Marie-Cappel on the Wednesday morning to see the mutinous B Flight. Read was gratified to note: 'Lubbock apologised to me for the whole affair and the matter was washed out and settled.' The revolt had had no effect on operations because mist had kept the squadron grounded, as it would for two days more. It was also bitterly cold and snow had turned the airfield to mush, promising to make landing perilous when flying resumed.

The squadron's riggers started cutting holes in the floors of the observers' cockpits so cameras could be fixed rigidly to take vertical pictures. More and more of the squadron's time was being devoted to photographic reconnaissance. The work was dangerous enough but because Strutters were designated as fighter-reconnaissance aircraft, the staff thought they should be able to take care of themselves and did not need scout escorts. Read's unsuccessful demands for escorts to be provided put him on a collision course with his superiors once again. The clear skies necessary for good photos left the slow Sopwiths vulnerable to attack. German scouts would sometimes allow the British to reach their furthest point east then as soon as they turned for home would dive out of the sun. To be fair, with photographic trips often extending deep into enemy territory, the RFC's Sopwith Pups and Nieuports would have been unable to accompany Strutters all the way because the two-seaters' four-hour endurance much exceeded theirs. The chief problem was that by this time the Strutter was becoming outclassed as a combat machine. It was graceful enough to look at, pleasant to fly and having a gun firing through the propeller had been a major advance when it first arrived in France in mid-1916. But too few were delivered too slowly and by early 1917 things had moved on. The Strutter, never really a dog-fighter, was coming up against the latest Albatros scout, the DIII or Vee Strutter. It was lighter and smaller yet considerably more powerful than the British machine. Crucially, it had twin, forward-firing machine-guns so packed a heftier punch. No 45 Squadron's crews could only soldier on. Lubbock and Belgrave, men of skill and nerve, had proved that an initial show of aggression could give a pilot the advantage of surprise and an opportunity to fire. Also the Strutters – No 45 Squadron's were identified by a vertical band round the fuselage and B Flight's sported white wheel covers – still had a nasty sting in the tail if a pilot manoeuvred rapidly to give his observer a good field of fire. In fact, the observer's Lewis on its moveable mounting was often the more useful of the Strutter's two guns. It would become apparent that the Strutter crews' best chance of survival was to keep in tight formation so that mutual covering fire could be provided from the rear cockpits. A classic error of the inexperienced pilot was to dive steeply away from an attacker on a straight course, leaving his gunner powerless because the tail was in the way of his firing. Whatever the tactics employed, the Strutter had had its day. The casualty toll for No 45 Squadron was bound to rise.

Belgrave saw no further action in February. He was rostered for photographic escort duty with Thompson on the 26th but the engine of A1086 was vibrating so badly that they could not take off. Belgrave made himself unpopular with the ground crew the following afternoon when he taxied out in A1072 for a test flight. The machine tipped on its nose, probably because it was caught in the slipstream of another aircraft. The propeller was smashed and the cowl damaged. On the last day of the month pilots were sent up for firing practice, using a nearby pond as the target. Belgrave took up 2/AM Burnaby Perrott but had to come back as A1086's engine was vibrating again due to bearing trouble.

Belgrave had now completed three months with the squadron and on March 2 he was sent on leave for two weeks. It would have given him ample time to return home to Chinnor and that may well be what he did. However, it is known that at some point during his service with the RFC he spent time on leave at Le Touquet. Wherever it was that he went to relax, the break gave Belgrave chance to unwind and chat to people with no direct knowledge of the life he had temporarily left behind. He would never have dreamed of 'line-shooting' about his exploits over the Front – that was considered the height of bad form – but he had every reason for quiet pride in a difficult and dangerous job well done. In his brief time at No 45 he had matured into one of its finest combat pilots. Belgrave was back at Ste-Marie-Cappel on March 15, his return coinciding with a visit from General Hugh 'Boom' Trenchard, who had taken over from Henderson as commander of the RFC in France in August 1915. During Belgrave's fourteen days away five close comrades, including Lubbock, had been killed and another invalided out, never to return.

Denys Greenhow had been the first to die. On March 6 he was observer to John Mackay in A1072, one of three Strutters led by Lubbock as they crossed the lines near St Eloi to take photographs. Mackay's engine gave trouble and he was forced to turn back. Pilot and observer were caught unawares when, between the lines and Houthulst Forest, they saw what they took to be five friendly aircraft. The machines were, in fact, Siemens Schuckert DIs, German copies of the Allies' Nieuport. They attacked and the Strutter was riddled with bullets. Wings and fuselage were extensively holed, a longeron was almost smashed, the tyres punctured and control wires severed. Greenhow was mortally wounded. Mackay, who narrowly escaped death when a bullet ripped his helmet, dived away and landed the Sopwith at No 41 Squadron's airfield at Abeele. Greenhow died minutes later. He was 19. Mackay went to hospital with severe shock and did not return to the squadron. Lubbock and Marshall, who was piloting the third Sopwith, had carried on unaware of Mackay's desperate plight. Lubbock was in his replacement aircraft A1082 with Thompson as observer as Austin was on leave. The Germans caught up with the remaining pair of Strutters and again were initially mistaken for friendly Nieuports. They attacked from above and behind. Eventually Thompson and Marshall's observer 2/AM Perrott, opened fire. One of the hostile aircraft broke away, but the other two dived under the Sopwiths, allowing Lubbock and Marshall to bring their front guns into play. Marshall's trigger cable to the Vickers' firing bar broke while he was firing but he pressed the knuckle joint and kept firing. One of the enemy aeroplanes dived away and crashed in the enemy lines but it was impossible to say who had shot it down. Marshall made it home in A1086 but the engine of Lubbock's A1082 packed up and, trying to reach Abeele, he crash-landed just short of the airfield.

With the death of Greenhow, only Lubbock and Austin remained of the original B Flight. The day after the fight, Read took Lubbock, Marshall and Mackay in his car to Greenhow's funeral at Lijssenthoek outside Poperinghe. A tender took more officers and a bearer party made up of B Flight members. As Lubbock joined the others in honouring a fallen comrade, fate was about to deal a cruel hand. The 'tiger' of No 45 Squadron had only four days to live. Lubbock was scheduled to take B Flight for a week's gunnery course at Cormont and he and Marshall went ahead by road on March 8 to make arrangements. Next day Wing HQ decided to send A Flight instead and the two officers returned to Ste-Marie-Cappel. On March 11 the snow and rain which had been hampering flying cleared for A Flight to fly to Cormont. Instead of the relatively relaxing prospect of a period of instruction, Lubbock found himself leading a line patrol in the repaired A1082. His observer Thompson, again standing in for Austin, was briefed to take photographs. They had Marshall and Truscott with them and in a third Sopwith was the less seasoned crew of 2nd Lt Horace Bowden and 2nd Lt Douglas Stevenson. Bowden, from Reigate, Surrey, had been with the squadron as a pilot since the previous October but had been sick for much of the time. Stevenson, educated at Christ's Hospital and King's College, London, had joined in early February, having served previously in the Duke of Cornwall's Light Infantry. For four of the six men taking to the air at 9.30am that Sunday it was their last mission.

Minutes after take-off Marshall landed in a field with a broken engine rocker arm, leaving the other Sopwiths to carry on as a pair. They began their patrol at 10.15am and shortly after 11am they were attacked over the Ypres salient by two Albatros DIIIs of Jasta 18. Troops in the British trenches saw the fight and reported that one of the enemy aircraft fell into the German lines. That is a mystery because neither German aeroplane was damaged and it was the two outclassed Strutters which were shot down in a combat lasting five minutes. Lubbock's machine broke up and went into a nose dive, its tattered fabric trailing. The Sopwith hit the ground just behind the Allied trenches near Railway Wood, outside Ypres. The victor was Leutnant Paul Strähle, who was just four days younger than Lubbock. The Sopwith was the second of Strähle's eventual total of fifteen claims. He survived active service throughout both World Wars to die in 1985. Bowden was shot through the head by Leutnant Josef Flink. As the British pilot slumped over the controls of A1071 the machine lurched into a series of violent, uncontrolled manoeuvres. It nose-dived, the wings folded back and the wreckage plunged into the moat at Ypres. Both observers were killed, falling from their cockpits as their machines went down. German gunners shelled the wreckage of Lubbock's aircraft but his body was retrieved by the Army. Five plates exposed by Thompson were also salvaged. Bowden's body was recovered when his smashed Strutter was hauled out of the moat. All the bodies were taken to No 10 Casualty Clearing Station at Poperinghe. That night the squadron carpenters made coffins and affixed brass plates engraved with ranks and names. Next afternoon all available officers from the squadron and most of B Flight were there to see a Canadian padre, Captain (Reverend) J J Callan, officiate as the four were buried alongside Greenhow. Lubbock was 23, Thompson and Stevenson 21 and Bowden only 20. The loss of Lubbock, in particular, was a great blow to the squadron. At the time of his death he was easily the squadron's most experienced combat pilot yet, although he had probably shot down several enemy aircraft, there was no record of a positive victory until March 6. Part of the reason was the inferior machinery with which he had to fight. Part was perhaps due to Lubbock's modesty in claiming success. 'A most gallant officer,' Read noted in his diary, dismissing his own previous reservations. 'He stood out immeasurably superior to all the other pilots in the squadron, good as most of them are.'

It is easy to give the impression that the Ste-Marie-Cappel to which Belgrave returned three days after the funerals was a place of unremitting gloom, a place where those lucky enough to escape the horrific death that could come, literally, out of the blue, were condemned to a life of chilly boredom and discomfort amid a quagmire. Yet there were attempts to brighten the existence of officers and men. During February a concert was held in the men's mess hut with senior officers from Wing and No 6 Squadron invited, Read sent a team of officers to Abeele to play No 6 at rugby and a boxing tournament was organised. In March the squadron's football team played when weather interfered with flying. On the 17th the team beat HQ 11th Wing 3-0 though there was some muttering as Read was the referee. The inevitable rematch, with another referee, resulted in a 6-0 victory for the squadron. Norman Macmillan, who joined the squadron at the end of March, recalled in *Into The Blue* how entertainment in the small wooden officers' mess was provided by a wind-up gramophone. 2nd Lt Charles Carleton brought records of Schubert, Madame Butterfly or tunes such as The Cobbler's Song from Chu Chin Chow, the hit musical of the day. There were also live acts. Lt Arthur Selby could rattle out impromptu tunes on the piano and another officer was a talented violinist. Solomon, thought to be the only Jewish pilot to fly with No 45 in the Great War, was a skilful exponent of the one-string fiddle – the jamboogoo, as the officers dubbed it. If some notes from this strange instrument proved a little painful someone would stuff a rag into the horn that acted as amplifier. If no one had the inclination for a sing-song there were always letters to write or bridge to be played.

When life around camp became too monotonous the fliers would commandeer a tender to take them to sample the drink and company in Bailleul or St Omer. Bailleul, an important railhead and supply centre with several squadrons based on its outskirts, was ten miles to the south-east of Ste-Marie-Cappel. Officers were forbidden to enter any but eight named restaurants or estaminets, one of which was called Madame Salome. An estaminet called The Soldiers' Rest was out of bounds to all ranks for reasons Macmillan neglected to explain. In St Omer one of the hotels was a recognised meeting place for the RFC. Friends from other squadrons within striking distance met over dinner and drinks and exchanged invitations to visit. Booze was the universally accepted antidote to the stresses of squadron life but any sensible pilot soon realised that moderation was all because flying into battle with reactions blunted by a hangover was a guaranteed way to shorten one's life. Virtually everyone smoked pipes or cigarettes. Macmillan was reticent about the circumstances in which his comrades sought female company. Read gave a hint when he noted how an officer – not one named in this book – was stricken with a 'distressing complaint' that needed hospital treatment. 'Damned fool,' was the CO's terse comment.

On March 17 Belgrave had a mishap when he took up a new observer, Lt J Scott, for practice. He had to make a forced landing outside the aerodrome and bent his machine. Early next morning he took up A2384 to escort a photo-reconnaissance flight but it was a washout, low cloud forcing a return after fifteen minutes. By 4.30pm the weather had cleared enough for Belgrave to join a patrol in the same aircraft. He came back, having scored his second victory by shooting down a German two-seater in flames to the north-east of Ploegsteert Wood. If Belgrave looked on the success as part revenge for the four men killed one week before, there is no hint of his feelings in a letter he wrote about the encounter.

He related: 'Three of us were on a patrol. Just as we were going home Courtney (*Frank Courtney, who joined No 45 in November 1916, had just been promoted Captain*) went towards some white Archie over the trenches. I saw the machines some miles off and watched him carefully. Courtney turned away, so did the other fellow so I fired a red light, which neither of them saw, and manoeuvred for position. I had plenty of height to spare but neither of us (Truscott was with me as observer) were quite certain if he was a Hun or not. I saw the markings when directly behind his tail, and still obviously unobserved (though he was a two-seater). Then of course I pushed the nose down. At about one hundred yards I opened fire and kept it up to about twenty yards, firing about three hundred shots in all. I saw the observer stand up and fire at us, but either he was hit at once or else was wildly excited as no bullets touched my machine. Then the Hun turned and we saw smoke coming out of his machine. He went down over Hunland, well alight, Truscott giving him a parting burst of fire as he came past our machine from fifteen yards' range.'

A postcript written the following day said: 'Last night the Archie battery in the region of our scrap phoned through and officially confirmed our Hun. They watched him go down in flames until he disappeared behind trees.' The next few days seemed relatively uneventful to Belgrave after such drama. On March 24 there was a long reconnaissance escort duty and on the following day he and Truscott in A2384 climbed over Wervicq with two other Sopwiths to seek a reported Zeppelin. They saw nothing above or below the clouds and returned. The weather was poor and a concert was held on March 26 in an attempt to brighten things up. Belgrave's aircraft were still plagued by engine trouble. On March 28 he had to abandon a reconnaissance flight when a cylinder seized on A2384. Swapping to A1092 for another try later in the day proved futile. Two rocker arms broke as he was running up the engine to test the power and he did not leave the ground. Crosses for Greenhow, Lubbock, Thompson, Bowden and Stevenson had been made by squadron craftsmen. The following day a tender took Belgrave with Austin and Truscott the ten miles to the cemetery so that they could erect the crosses on the graves. Belgrave would soon assume Lubbock's mantle as No 45's premier combat pilot. From uncertain new boy to respected stalwart in four months; such was the pace of life, and death, in a front-line squadron. Norman Macmillan calculated that by the end of March the squadron had lost twenty-two fliers killed, missing or wounded, about one a week and equal to the total who had first arrived in France. Read still considered that many of the replacements arriving were pretty poor and even succeeded in having some sent back home. Despite this the squadron had by and large overcome its shaky start.

The RFC was entering what became known as Bloody April. For the Corps, and the Royal Naval Air Service, it was to be worst month of the entire war with 319 aircrew lost, 252 of them killed or taken prisoner. Much of the slaughter was down to the demands of providing air support for the Battle of Arras launched early that month. The RFC still did not have the machines it needed and was facing Jastas honed into fine fighting units. The Germans, having discarded their policy of mainly defensive tactics behind their own lines, were to enjoy an ascendancy in the air perhaps greater than at any other time in the war. Most of the action was south of No 45's patch; nevertheless the squadron did not get through April unscathed. The month got off to a bad start for Belgrave. Sunday the 1st was marked by scudding cloud and rain and when he did take advantage of a brief spell of finer weather to get airborne his engine seized and he had to make a forced landing, badly bending his machine in a ditch. The Sopwith was taken to No 1 Aircraft Depot for repair next day. It was concluded that the still-snowy weather was causing the castor oil then used as engine lubricant to freeze in oil pumps overnight. The problem could be avoided by using hot compresses, something that B Flight had been neglecting to do. On April 3, after an overnight blizzard, Belgrave took off with eight other machines but had to return with yet more engine bother. The others turned back due to the weather. Another washout.

Good Friday, April 6, was a black day for the squadron. Six fliers, including Truscott, the observer who had shared Belgrave's victory the previous month, were killed in action. Nine Sopwiths left Ste-Marie-Cappel soon after 9am on a photographic mission deep into enemy territory. One turned back with engine trouble. Another was wrecked when it crashed after making it back to the lines with a propeller blade blown off by anti-aircraft fire. The crew was not badly hurt. The remaining seven aircraft pressed on, only to be attacked by six German machines. The British held formation and beat off the aggressors. Six Albatros DIIIs of Jasta 30 based at Phalempin then arrived on the scene to boost the enemy force. The outnumbered British were turning home over Tournai, having completed the photography, when the Germans struck again. 2nd Lt James Blake and Captain William Brayshay, who had joined the mission in 7806 as a reserve crew, were shot down and killed. Blake, aged 24, was from Darlington. Brayshay, from Birmingham, was three weeks short of his 30th birthday. They fell under the guns of Jasta 30's commander Oberleutnant Hans Bethge, a 26-year-old Berliner. The rest of the formation, led by Captain McArthur, weaved, dived and zoomed but it was of little use against the superior DIIIs. In the mêlée two of the Sopwiths collided. Frank Courtney saw it happen. The right wing of Marshall's A1093 suddenly folded up, perhaps as a result of a long-range fluke shot from one of the Germans hitting the rigging. The stricken Sopwith twisted violently and crashed into 2nd Lt Campbell's A2381. Bits flew in all directions, narrowly missing the tail of Courtney's Strutter, as the wrecked machines plunged to earth at Pecq, east of Roubaix. Marshall and Truscott, his observer, died, as did Campbell and his observer Captain Donald Edwards. Colin Campbell, a doctor's son from Toronto, had trained as a mining engineer. He was 34. Edwards, from London, was 26. The four were credited to Leutnant Joachim von Bertrab, of Jasta 30, who had already accounted for two Martinsydes in his purple Albatros that day. One of the German aircraft was shot down when 2nd Lt John Murison, observer to 2nd Lt Geoffrey Cock in A1075, fired fifty rounds into it at thirty yards' range. Murison, a volunteer from the Machine Gun Corps, was an extrovert who prided himself on his talents with the Lewis. 2/AM Perrott, gunner to Lt Philip Newling, drove down another German aircraft out of control. The four remaining Sopwiths fought their way home with eleven exposed plates. It seemed a poor bargain – six good men and four aeroplanes for just eleven photographs of objectives. Von Bertrab was shot down by Britain's greatest ace Mick Mannock on August 12 that year and taken prisoner.

Courtney later recalled a tragicomedy aspect of the grim affair. Truscott, as B Flight's mess president, was entrusted with the bundles of francs that constituted the mess funds. As he prepared for what was to be his last flight Truscott made a big show of shoving a fat envelope into the pocket of his flying coat, telling everyone it was his 'insurance' against being shot down. He reckoned that if his comrades saw him under attack they would go to his aid rather than see their funds vanish. Courtney admitted that when Truscott fell to his fate the thought flashed through his mind 'What about our mess money?' Then another dogfight erupted and Courtney had no time to think of anything else. When he and his observer Austin finally walked into the mess hut after their exhausting ordeal a Corporal came up with a fat envelope and said: 'Mr Truscott told me to give you this if he didn't come back this evening.'

It was unfortunate for Courtney that Brigadier General Tom Webb-Bowen, commander of 2nd Brigade RFC, under which No 45 Squadron served, had chosen that disastrous day to visit Ste-Marie-Cappel. The General made some remark which seemed to suggest that the squadron's fliers were not fighting with enough determination. With six dead comrades in mind, Courtney objected out loud, though whether his protest was meant to be heard by Webb-Bowen is uncertain. The General said nothing at the time but within three weeks Courtney was on his way home. On April 7 Courtney braved the cloud and rain to fly Belgrave to No 1 Aircraft Depot to pick up a new Strutter, 7762. Belgrave had a frustrating time of it the following day. First he had to drop out of a patrol because his machine was vibrating. Then a line patrol he and Austin were flying in A2382 was cut short by cloud. Easter Monday, April 9, saw the officers losing 3-2 to the squadron team in a football game played partly in a blizzard. As No 45 Squadron struggled in the mud of a soccer pitch a more serious contest was being fought and won 30 miles to the south. Canadian troops stormed and secured Vimy Ridge and the British also made good gains when the infantry phase of the Battle of Arras got under way. The Ridge had been in German hands since October 1914. Its capture meant the Allies could look down on the Douai plain from its 200ft high slopes. News of the famous victory reached Ste-Marie-Cappel from GHQ next day.

Winter refused to release its grip as April continued. The cold, wind and rain was reflected in Read's bleak mood. He thought his men had battled brilliantly on April 6 and received no thanks from Wing in return. His requests for scout escorts for the sitting-duck Strutters still fell on deaf ears. Read was also still carping about the quality of pilots sent to him. Aeroplanes continued to be damaged with monotonous regularity in forced landings, and labour troubles in England delayed the supply of replacement machines. The squadron strength of aircraft fell to twelve. As a stop-gap, Nieuport 20s were allocated to the squadron, the first two being flown in from St Omer on April 13. That day Belgrave, with 2nd Lt Charles Stewart as observer in Strutter A1080, escorted a photo-reconnaissance patrol as far as the lines. They spotted one enemy aircraft in the distance but returned without incident. Back at Ste-Marie-Cappel Belgrave joined the other pilots in examining the Nieuports and was not impressed. High winds over the next two days prevented the Nieuports being tried out properly but training started on the 16th and four days later the squadron had seven of the machines, Belgrave having fetched one of them himself. The verdict was that they were dud. The Nieuports were French two-seaters, similar in concept to the Strutter, but of an earlier and even less combat-worthy design. They had become available because No 46 squadron was getting rid of theirs to re-equip with Sopwith Pups. The Nieuports were even slower than the sluggish Strutters and only demonstrated any manoeuvrability when they tumbled into an unwanted spin. The view from the cockpit was poor and the controls heavy. The Le Rhône engines were better than the Strutters' Clergêts and the Nieuports had stronger undercarriages but there was little else in their favour. Each flight was allocated two of the machines and at first they were kept for training newly-arrived pilots. At least that way they were useful because Strutters could be reserved for combat without having to suffer undue wear and tear from clumsy tyros. When the Nieuports were used on operations they were confined to line patrols and oblique photography of German positions from a safe distance. It would have been foolhardy in the extreme to send them deep into enemy territory. Willie Read himself dismissed the Nieuports as artillery observation machines unfit for the work expected of No 45 Squadron, although this did not prevent him expressing displeasure at what he saw as unnecessary grousing by B and C Fights at having been lumbered with the duds.

Meanwhile, on April 14, the squadron was turfed out of its relatively comfortable quarters to move to a tent city on the other side of the airfield. The reason was the imminent arrival at Ste-Marie-Cappel of No 20 Squadron which, perhaps because it was the senior unit, was allocated the better accommodation. Four canvas-covered Bessonneau hangars were erected for No 45. Each operational flight's mess was in a marquee and the squadron headquarters flight mess had to make do with an Army bell tent. Wooden huts were put up for headquarters and photographic use and pit props were laid as hardstanding for workshop lorries. No 20's advance guard of tenders drove in on the 15th and its FE2d pushers landed from Boisdinghem the following day. Belgrave and his comrades were less than pleased at having to live and sleep under canvas without even floorboards to cover the wet grass that cold spring. Yet there was no animosity towards No 20, a fine squadron, and friendly relations were soon established. Read hoped that having a fighter squadron as a close neighbour might make it possible to arrange escorts for his Strutters at last. Indeed on the 16th of the month six of No 20's aircraft were detailed to accompany six Strutters on an operation but the weather prevented it and the two squadrons rarely flew together. No 45 was grounded by rain, snow and hail on April 17 and only rapid work with lashing ropes prevented the wind blowing away B Flight's hangar. Over the next couple of days the skies cleared sufficiently for Belgrave to fit in some practice flying. He took part in two photo-reconnaissance flights on April 23, St George's Day, though one was cut short by the weather. The following day, blessed for a change with fine spring weather, he took up a new observer, Lt Dudley Eglington, a pre-war Guys' freshman, for a familiarisation flight in one of the Nieuports. There was a little more excitement for Belgrave later in the day when he was on a photo-reconnaissance with 2nd Lt Stewart in A1080. Three enemy aircraft were spotted and the British formation engaged one of them briefly but the encounter was inconclusive. Belgrave would have to wait until the following month to add to his tally.

Back on the ground, Belgrave prepared to meet his new commanding officer. Willie Read had had enough. Frustrated, disillusioned and anxious to confront the enemy personally, he had applied to return to the cavalry. Read had completed precisely one year as squadron commander. He was sickened by the heavy losses sustained, particularly as he had been denied the right to lead his men in the air and was unsuccessful in persuading higher authority to provide escorts. Read had seen the loss of just about the entire squadron strength in six months in return for a few confirmed victories. The irony was that, as he left, the squadron was on the brink of worthwhile success, thanks in great part to his training programme. He would not be there to see the fruits of his efforts. Read had to drop rank from Major to temporary Captain to return to the 1st Dragoon Guards, who were then near Albert. His ambition to lead cavalry into action would not be realised and after four months of virtually static warfare he was begrudgingly accepted back into the RFC where he had a successful career.

The squadron's new CO was Major Pierre Helperus Andrias Van Ryneveld, a South African with extensive flying experience in Palestine and Salonika and on home defence in the UK. He had the MC and the yellow and blue ribbon of the Egyptian Order of the Nile, rumoured to be for landing in the face of the enemy to rescue a fellow pilot who had force-landed. Van Ryneveld had spent a few days with Read, and they were seen strolling from the headquarters office to the workshops, hangars and HQ mess deep in conversation. When the handover came on April 24 Read left without ceremony. There was a great contrast in appearance and styles of the two men. Van Ryneveld, of Cape Dutch stock, was eight inches taller than Read who was about 5ft 4ins. He would also try to work around the obstructive staffs rather than take them head-on as Read had done. Belgrave joined other pilots and observers when the new CO called them together. In his Boer accent, he quietly urged them to do their best and promised what support he could provide. He had had model aeroplanes made out of bullets threaded on wires projecting from wooden stands. With these Van Ryneveld explained his ideas on formations and fighting tactics. On the vexed question of escorts, he was realistic. He told the fliers that he knew the COs of scout squadrons and would ask them to tell their pilots to keep a look-out whenever they were due on patrol across the lines at the same time as No 45. He did manage to informally arrange for No 1 Squadron's Nieuports, based at Bailleul, to provide cover if they were about when the Sopwiths were operating. Van Ryneveld did not pretend there would be a great improvement; inter-squadron co-ordination would remain largely a matter of chance. The Strutters would have to continue to rely on their disciplined formations. Neverthless, the new CO made a good impression on Belgrave and the others. Van Ryneveld made a point of briefing missions himself as often as possible. He was banned from flying over the lines, as Read had been, but often climbed into an aircraft on the pretext of checking the weather in the hope of encountering a hostile intruder. He tangled with enemy two-seaters four times. Incidentally, No 45 was not the only squadron battling to make the most of the Strutters' capabilities on photo-reconnaissance tasks; No 70 and No 43 Squadrons were similarly equipped.

The last day of the month brought another loss. 2nd Lt William Wright, with 2/AM Perrott as his gunner, was in A1080 escorting a morning photo-reconnaissance when, near Armentières, the Strutter was singled out by Jasta 28's Leutnant Max Ritter von Müller. The Sopwith crew put up a good fight against the 30-year-old Bavarian former locksmith's apprentice but Perrott was shot in the head. Oundle-educated Wright, aged 21, who had served in the Leicestershire Regiment, managed to get back across the lines and land at Lillers, to find his gunner dead in the rear cockpit.

May saw a fresh start. Not only was there a new CO but brighter weather brought more opportunity for the squadron to prove itself. The Nieuports were ferried back to St Omer early in the month, to everyone's relief, and Strutters with Clergêts giving an extra 20hp over the old engines started to arrive. The month would also be Belgrave's most successful with the squadron, a time when he was able to demonstrate his fighting qualities in indisputable fashion. For the first few days he was teamed regularly with 2nd Lt Stewart as his observer in A2382. On May 1 they were one of five crews escorting four more on a photo-reconnaissance. The formation tangled with one enemy aircraft, which was forced to land, though Belgrave was not directly involved. An early-morning offensive patrol the following day came across no Germans. Belgrave and Stewart were again on escort duty that afternoon when three enemy machines were engaged, without any decisive result. On May 3 the pair were on an offensive patrol when they were surprised to see a small, pear-shaped balloon over Poperinghe at 12,000ft with apparently nothing attached to it. Another uneventful offensive patrol completed their day's duties. On May 4 they were on patrol in A6741, one of the despised Nieuports, two days before it was returned. They followed two hostile aircraft from Armentières to Ypres but their hopeless machine would not climb and Belgrave was forced to turn for home anyway as he was stricken by cramp in his right leg. Back in A2382 on May 5, Belgrave was rewarded with his third victory. At 11.45am he and Stewart were part of an offensive patrol at 10,000ft over Becelaere in the north of No 45 Squadron's sector. Belgrave was the first to spot five or six Albatros DIIIs and Halberstadts flying south-west towards Ploegsteert. He dived under his patrol leader and fired a red light to direct his attention to the enemy aircraft, which were higher and behind the Sopwiths. Belgrave, temporarily out of formation, climbed back towards the Germans, two of which dived to the attack while the others maintained their height. Belgrave opened fire on one of the Germans then turned to attack another. He got under the tail of this machine and was able to get in a long burst at close range. He recounted later: 'The HA started a spin, rolled over and fell past us out of control. There still remained two HA above us, one of which was attacking. We turned towards him and the observer fired at him at close range but was unable to make good shooting because of the top plane. The other hostile machine was then drawing up over the tail, but was driven down under control.' Sergeant Ernest Cook and his observer 1/AM Lambert in A1075 also played their part in driving off the Germans by opening fire. As Belgrave's victim, a light coloured Albatros with red ailerons and elevators, plunged to earth, the Sopwiths reformed. They continued to circle over enemy territory, attracting heavy fire from German anti-aircraft batteries. The two German aeroplanes followed for a while, keeping out of reach before eventually turning east. The Sopwiths headed for base.

Belgrave notched up his fourth victory on May 7 when he and his observer Stewart were part of an offensive patrol. They were at 10,000ft near Lille at 6.45pm when they saw two Albatros scouts 1,000ft below them. A further five were 1,000ft above but further away. Belgrave pushed down the nose of A2382 and closed on one of the lower German machines, firing a long burst from his Vickers. He then positioned to allow Stewart a short burst but the Albatros dived away to safety. Disappointed, Belgrave reformed with other patrol members to engage the remaining six Germans. 'After this we had so many short engagements that it is difficult to say where one began and the other ended and it was impossible to watch what other machines were doing,' he said, summing up the utter confusion of a mass dog fight. At one stage Belgrave dived firing on one Albatros DIII, which burst into flames and went straight down. There was no time to dwell on the fate of the enemy pilot in his doomed machine or watch his descent because several of the German's comrades dived towards the Sopwith. Stewart managed to land hits on two of them. Two other Germans were sent down out of control, one by Cock and Murison and the other by 2nd Lt Carleton, who had John Vessey as observer. Soon only two enemy aircraft remained nearby and, although they had the advantage of height, they turned away as soon as two of the Sopwiths made for them. Stewart tried a parting shot at long range with no real hope of achieving anything. The combat was over. On the way home, with no Vickers ammunition left and only half a drum left for the Lewis, Belgrave and Stewart joined an attack on a kite balloon over Wervicq and it was rapidly pulled down. Belgrave then saw one of the other Sopwiths dive on an enemy aircraft. Tracers plainly struck home and the German went into a vertical dive, 'at a ghastly speed' as Belgrave noted, but further accounts of that incident have not come to light.

Whatever depths of fear Belgrave and his colleagues had felt during their battle that evening, whatever exhilaration at their victories, whatever degree of thankfulness swept over them as they returned safely, it was all as nothing compared to the astonishing experiences of two of their comrades earlier in the day. 2nd Lt Harry Forrest and his gunner 1/AM Lambert were flying alone on a defensive patrol in A1075 when, after ninety minutes, the sight of British anti-aircraft fire near Dickebusch Lake directed them to a pair of enemy aircraft. The Sopwith struggled to climb to the same level as the Germans so Forrest passed two hundred feet beneath with the intention of letting Lambert fire his Lewis upwards into them. He assumed the AA gunners would cease fire as soon as they saw what he was up to. He was wrong. Lambert had fired a few bursts at one of the German machines when his Lewis jammed and at the same moment an AA shell hit the Strutter, followed by another. The shells did not explode as they were time-fused but damaged the tailplane and rear fuselage, severing all the control lines leading to the tail. Forrest was robbed of any means of controlling his machine's pitch and it went into a dive. The rapid increase in speed sent it climbing into a loop, a manoeuvre never experienced by the pilot or observer, and then another. At this stage four 97-round ammunition drums for the Lewis broke free and slid inside the fuselage towards the rear, where they lodged. The transfer of weight was sufficient to restore some balance to the stricken Sopwith. But with 2,000ft already lost in the loops, the machine embarked on a stomach-churning series of zooms, stalls and dives as it fell another 7,000ft. It is difficult to imagine the terror and feelings of wretched hopelessness with which Forrest and Lambert battled as they clung on during the nightmare descent, lasting anything from eight to fifteen minutes, waiting for the inevitable. But by great luck the aeroplane hit the ground as it had almost finished pulling out of one of its dives. The wheels hit a fence and the Strutter cartwheeled over it and fell into a disused gun-pit. Both men clambered from the wreckage near Ouderdom in British territory unhurt but deeply shocked. Forrest was sent home for a long rest. Lambert stayed with the squadron but transferred to ground duties as an armourer. It seems their appalling ordeal had not been totally in vain. The few rounds fired by Lambert had found their mark and one of the hostile aircraft was seen falling out of control, though its fate was not confirmed.

As Belgrave and his comrades unwound at Ste-Marie-Cappel and mulled over the day's events, they were unaware of another drama that had been played out in the rapidly fading light a little over 25 miles to the south-east. Albert Ball, 'star' of the RFC thanks to publicity he himself never courted, was seen chasing a red Albatros into a large bank of low cloud near Annoeulin. He had been in the air for three hours on that, his second flight of the day. Mentally and physically drained after being involved in several skirmishes, he probably became disoriented in the cloud for his SE5 emerged inverted barely 500ft above the ground. There was no chance of him righting his machine before it smashed into the ground in German-held territory. Ball, only 20, died in the arms of a French girl who ran to the wreckage. His posthumous Victoria Cross was gazetted on June 8. The citation said Captain Ball had destroyed forty-three German aeroplanes and one balloon in all – which raises the vexed question of 'kills' and 'victories'. Researchers have established that Ball triumphed over sixty-seven enemy aircraft and balloons though no one suggests, and Ball certainly never did, that these were all destroyed. The figures include many aircraft listed as being driven down out of control, thoroughly defeated but whose end was not actually witnessed. A pilot engaged in a dog fight could not afford to watch his opponent's descent all the way to the ground if he wanted to avoid being 'jumped' himself so he would not know whether the enemy managed to recover sufficiently to make a survivable forced landing or indeed whether he had been feigning all along merely to escape. Neverthless it seems justifiable to list these claims as victories as they certainly put an enemy out of the fray, at least temporarily. For this reason, in calculating Belgrave's tally, claims of aircraft out of control have been taken into account.

Two days after Ball's death No 45 Squadron suffered its own losses in its first full-scale engagement of May. On the evening of the 9th Captain McArthur was in A8226 leading an offensive patrol of six Strutters when they were attacked by a dozen or so Albatros single-seaters of Jasta 28 between Menin and Warneton. Lawrence McArthur, a 26-year-old Irishman who had been with the squadron since its earliest days, had to dive for the safety of Bailleul airfield after his rigging wires were shot away. His observer Senior was mortally wounded but, despite his right hand being partly shot away, he bravely kept up his fire with his left hand and managed to drive down one of the Germans. Despite the damage to the Sopwith, McArthur threw it into a spin to evade two other attackers. His aircraft held together and after McArthur pulled off a safe landing Senior was rushed to the nearby hospital but died a few days later. Senior, who was 24, came from Wakefield, West Yorkshire. At Clare College, Cambridge, he had been a prize-winning classics scholar before joining the West

Yorks Regiment (Prince of Wales's Own) from which he transferred to the RFC. Britain could ill afford to lose men of his calibre. McArthur, although he had found aerial victories elusive, was of undoubted gallantry. He held the Military Cross for action with the infantry in 1915 when, badly wounded, he had rallied retiring troops and held a trench under heavy fire. Norman Macmillan rated him 'a fine type', recalling his 'stout courage, even temper, good humour and great kindliness'.The clash with Jasta 28, flying from its base at Marcke-sur-Lys between Courtrai and Menin, also resulted in the death of one of No 45's newcomers, 19-year-old Lt William Mills. His 7803 attracted the fire of the experienced 25-year-old Leutnant Karl Schäfer, who had taken over command of Jasta 28 a fortnight previously. Mills slumped over his controls badly wounded and the Strutter fell out of control. He died within hours of the crash. His observer 2/AM J W Loughlin was thrown clear on impact and, although he suffered a foot injury, he survived the war as a prisoner. Mills, a former regular in the artillery and observer with No 8 Squadron, had gained his pilot's wings only the previous month. Loughlin, formerly an Army private, had been with No 45 for only six days as an air gunner on probation. The apparent ease with which the pair were shot down hammered home the merits of Read's policy of not sending new crews to face the enemy without letting them have one or two supervised sorties first. Perhaps Mills's time as an observer had been thought sufficient experience. Despite the losses, No 45 Squadron emerged victors of the scrap as Cock and his observer Murison in A8260 each destroyed an Albatros, though Murison had to share the credit for his with 2nd Lt Wright and Lt Edward Caulfield-Kelly in A8225. 2nd Lt James Johnstone and 2/AM Thomas Harries in A963 sent down another Albatros. The squadron had every reason to feel proud, having fought the engagement at odds of two to one against.

The long-awaited improvement in the weather which allowed this level of deadly activity in the sky at least made life on the ground a great deal more pleasant for Belgrave and his friends. The bell tent which served as squadron headquarters had been replaced by a wooden hut and, although the three operational flights still messed in marquees, floorboards had been supplied and the mud had dried up anyway. On warm days the flaps of officers' tents, which were pitched in a poplar-lined paddock, were rolled up to provide an airing. Camp beds were hauled out on to the grass so that officers could relax in the sunshine with only the occasional rumble of artillery from the closest sectors of the Front to disturb the peace. Dogs scampered underfoot. Although such pets were officially banned, the squadron usually had mutts in residence. One was a fox terrier called Beattie, perhaps because its fighting qualities matched those of the Admiral, and there was an alsatian bitch called Crash.

Belgrave had missed out on the action of May 9 and two days later an offensive patrol which he and Stewart joined in A2382 was cut short by thick cloud. There was more frustration on the morning of May 12 when, again paired with Stewart, Belgrave's Sopwith was one of three to drop out of a nine-aircraft offensive patrol with technical problems. Twenty minutes after landing back at Ste-Marie-Cappel, Belgrave was airborne again, this time in the hastily commandeered A1092. But his hopes of catching up with the patrol were thwarted as his replacement machine also developed engine trouble only five minutes after take-off. The six remaining aircraft were involved in a series of inconclusive clashes although one enemy machine crashed in flames. It was credited to 2nd Lt R S Watt and his observer, 25-year-old fellow Canadian Lt George Blaiklock, in A8173. Johnstone and Harries, in A963, were credited with forcing a two-seater Albatros CV to land on the British side of the lines. Belgrave had to content himself with flying 2nd Lt Wright over to No 1 Aircraft Depot to collect a new machine that evening. Even that took two attempts, thanks to A2382's reluctant engine. The aircraft performed well enough the following morning for Belgrave to complete a photo-reconnaissance. He saw three enemy aircraft sporting white markings but nothing came of the sighting. Then on May 14 the troublesome A2382 did its best to kill him during a routine hop to take Captain Christopher Jenkins to the depot to pick up another new Strutter. On the return trip Belgrave's rudder controls jammed in the air and he was lucky to land with only minor damage to the aircraft. He was on similar ferrying duties the following day, although in the somewhat more reliable A8280. Unknown to Belgrave, death had claimed another of his family that day, Tuesday May 15. His 24-year-old cousin Amyas Willis, a captain in the 4th Battalion Middlesex Regiment, had succumbed to wounds in hospital at Etaples. The two knew each other from boyhood days in Switzerland. Willis's mother Marion, sister of Belgrave's mother, was a widow and living in Surrey at the time of her son's death.

Bad weather prevented much flying over the next couple of days but Belgrave was in action on May 20 when the squadron had a scrap in which it again gave a fine account of itself despite being outnumbered. Belgrave, with Stewart as observer, was in A8280 on an afternoon offensive patrol with six other Sopwiths led by Captain Jenkins, who had joined the squadron on April 9 to command B flight. They encountered about ten, and possibly up to fifteen, Albatros and Halberstadt scouts at 11,000ft near Lille. Belgrave's own part in the ensuing clash was limited because his Vickers jammed soon after he opened fire on an enemy and he had to extricate himself from the combat long enough to cure the crossfeed. However, the redoubtable Geoffrey Cock, in A8226 with 2nd Lt Allan Carey, sent down one enemy aircraft out of control. Sergeant Cook and his observer Blaiklock in A8268 each shot down a German machine, a Halberstadt and an Albatros, in flames. But the outstanding performance of the day came from Jenkins' observer Lt Eglington.

Jenkins, who had previously served with the Royal Sussex Regiment, saw four or five of the enemy machines about five hundred yards away and led his formation at them. Having closed the gap to about two hundred yards, he opened fire at the nearest German. One Albatros dived almost vertically on his Strutter from about 2,000ft above and in front while two more Germans closed in from the right. Jenkins attempted to aim at the diving enemy as it closed on him rapidly, firing. The German aircraft was only about fifty yards away when it pulled out of its descent. Eglington emptied a drum of Lewis ammunition into the Albatros as it swooped over his head. It crumpled and fell out of control. Eglington, aged 21, had no chance to savour his success for at the same time Jenkins alerted him through the speaking tube that he had been hit. The Sopwith then lurched as its stricken pilot slumped unconscious over his controls. Eglington, from Maidenhead, Berks, climbed out of his cockpit, exposing himself to the full blast of the slipstream, and crawled along the fuselage to reach the lower wing, which was slippery with castor oil blown back from the engine. Clinging to one of the half struts with one hand, he reached in to grasp the pilot's control stick and keep the aircraft level. In that highly precarious position the observer managed to steer A8246 safely through the Archie and crash-landed behind the Allied trenches at Neuve Eglise. Eglington emerged from the wreckage unscathed though, sadly, 19-year-old Christopher Jenkins, from Ealing, West London, died of his wounds three days later. Dudley Eglington, who had been wounded twice during his two years with the Black Watch, was awarded the Military Cross for his astonishing feat of courage and coolness.

Geoffrey Cock's victory on the 20th was his fifth, including claims by his gunner, thus making him the squadron's first ace. Not bad for a chap who wore a monocle. The eye piece was no affectation – it was needed for one defective eye. Geoffrey Hornblower Cock, from Shrewsbury, was twice turned away by medical officers when he tried for a commission in the infantry. Undaunted, he bluffed his way past the medics to enter the 28th London Regiment (Artists' Rifles) Officers' Training Corps in 1915 and transferred to the RFC in June 1916. Tall and immaculate in uniform, 21-year-old Cock had a slight stutter. His courage and determination to defy the Strutter's limitations had made him formidable in combat. Belgrave had only four days to wait before he became the squadron's second ace, though there were more mundane matters to attend to first. On May 21 an offensive patrol was cut short, allowing him time to take the familiar ride to No 1 Aircraft Depot, so that 2nd Lt Arthur Dobson could collect a new machine. There was also an unpromising start to May 24 when, again teamed with Stewart in A8280, he joined three other Sopwiths on a morning offensive patrol. Four enemy aircraft were seen over Menin but the clouds were getting thicker. With visibility deteriorating and fuel running low after two and a half hours airborne, the flight headed for home. Belgrave had to wait until that evening for his fifth victory.

Belgrave, again with Stewart but this time in A8223, was a member of an offensive patrol which, after a little over an hour in the air, encountered nine enemy scouts over Zonnebeke at 7.45pm. He was soon involved in a deadly fight against pilots who, as he later acknowledged, manoeuvred their machines very skilfully. The dry, factual nature of Belgrave's combat report does not disguise the drama of the encounter at 9,500ft. He noted: 'I saw two formations of HA, one of five machines and one of about four. We turned and attacked the first formation, with the patrol. The HA were above us and between us and our lines. The HA dived at one of our machines and then the other formation joined in the fight. I saw one HA on the tail of a Sopwith and was able to get on to his tail and we opened fire at very close range indeed. The HA turned across my front and we narrowly avoided a collision. I then attacked him again at about thirty yards' range. The HA fell out of control and side-slipped, his nose finally going down vertically. After that we had become separated from our other machines and we had some very close fighting with a large number of the HA. Very early in this part of the combat my observer was wounded. We made for our lines with the HA in close pursuit. My observer though badly wounded was able to fire about three more drums at very close range. I do not know if he obtained any results. The HA pursued us closely until near Ypres. They then left us and I landed at No 1 Squadron's aerodrome.'

Stewart, with No 45 since the previous January, had been shot in the leg and, although he survived, it was the end of his career with the squadron. Belgrave and his gallant observer were credited with having driven down the aircraft, an Albatros DIII, out of control. They shared the victory with Lt Newling and Lt W E Holland in A1095 and 2nd Lt Wright's observer Lt Caulfield-Kelly in A8269. Earlier in the same engagement Caulfield-Kelly had already demonstrated his skill with a Lewis by shooting down another German in flames. As Wright later summed up the double victory: 'Rear gun got a close burst into one who passed over our machine and turned to dive. A large burst of smoke from HA. It crashed in flames. Another HA dived on us firing. Rear gun opened fire and the HA appeared to half turn and go down, evidently badly out of control. A third HA attacked at extraordinarily close range and we both had to give him immediate attention so could not follow the disappearing HA.' Newling and Holland, the latter having been with the squadron only a week, were lucky to get home as their machine was badly shot up. On a later sortie Captain Gordon Mountford and 2nd Lt Vessey drove down two more German machines out of control. The only casualty that day apart from Stewart was Frank Austin, Lubbock's former observer. On this occasion flying with Cock in A8279, he was wounded in the thigh when caught in anti-aircraft fire and was taken to hospital.

The Germans redressed the balance somewhat the following day when 2nd Lt James Johnstone and his observer 2nd Lt Thomas Millar were shot down in A963 near Langemarck by Vizefeldwebel (equivalent to Sergeant Major) Karolus Bärenfänger of Jasta 28. Johnstone, who was wounded, and Millar, with the squadron a week, were both taken prisoner. The loss of a crew could not interrupt the squadron routine, which found Belgrave taking three flights to give new pilot 2nd Lt Bernard Smith some combat tips and making the inevitable trip to No 1 Aircraft Depot to fetch new Strutter A1016. On May 26 Belgrave was on patrol with Caulfield-Kelly as observer when eight hostile aircraft were spotted but they were too high to be attacked. The following day would bring Belgrave his sixth victory and the squadron more success, though at a price. Early on the morning of May 27 Belgrave was on a long-distance offensive and photographic patrol with four other Strutters – there should have been five but one had to return, unable to reach formation height because of technical problems. His observer in A8280 was 2nd Lt Gwynonfryn Davies, who was about to see action on only his fourth day with the squadron. At 6.30am the Sopwiths encountered a number of Albatros scouts 11,000ft over Roulers and turned to the attack only to find more Germans joining the fray until there were about ten of them. Undaunted by odds of two to one, the British crews got the best of their opponents. Belgrave's combat report, in which he refers to himself in the third person, explains his part in the engagement: 'We attacked a formation of HA over Roulers. The HA withdrew to the east after being engaged. We then turned and attacked two other HA who were going east. The first formation joined in the fight again and several other HA also came up. We had a mixed fight for many minutes in which the pilot and observer both got in several long bursts at various HA at effective range. The pilot attacked one HA which was fighting a Sopwith and was able to get a short burst in at about fifty yards' range. The HA appeared to be hit but the pilot had to turn almost at once and so lost sight of him. Several pilots and observers in the formation saw this machine fall out of control.' Wright and his observer Carey confirmed seeing the Albatros DIII go down. Cock, with Caulfield-Kelly in A1016, sent another Albatros down out of control. Two more Germans dived vertically out of harm's way, one of them to escape the attentions of 2nd Lt Matthew 'Bunty' Frew, who opened fire at close range. Frew, whose observer was 2nd Lt M J Dalton, had joined the squadron only a month before and had yet to score a victory. After the 22-year-old Scot did open his account the following month he went on to become the squadron's highest scoring ace with twenty-three victories, a DSO and two MCs to his credit. It had been a successful morning, with the Strutters even returning with twelve exposed photographic plates.

A second patrol that day clashed with seven more Albatros scouts. One of the enemy aircraft was shot down by 2nd Lt Fitchat with 2nd Lt Reginald Hayes as his observer in A1099. Captain Mountford with 2nd Lt Vessey in A8299 drove down another out of control, as did Sergeant Cook with 2/AM Harry Shaw, from Clapton, London, in A8268. The squadron had notched up five victories in a day but with the loss of two of the dwindling band of fliers who had been with the squadron since 1916. Captain McArthur and his observer, 2nd Lt Allan Carey, were posted missing in A8226. They were last seen at 12,000ft about two miles east of the enemy lines. A few days later a German aircraft dropped a message confirming their deaths near Ypres. Carey had been teamed with McArthur after the loss of Senior, his previous observer. A8226 was the thirteenth victory for Leutnant von Müller of Jasta 28. The Bavarian would eventually achieve thirty-six victories and hold the Pour le Mérite, the coveted Blue Max, only to leap to his death from his blazing Albatros, a victim of No 21 Squadron, the following

January. On May 28 a patrol tangled with another large formation of Albatros scouts. Two Germans went down in flames, both falling to the guns of observers: Caulfield-Kelly, whose pilot in A8269 was Wright, and 2nd Lt Wilfred Corner, with Cock in A1095. Caulfield-Kelly was wounded but survived. Then on the last day of May there were two claims of enemy aircraft being driven down out of control, one by Mountford's observer Vessey and the other by 2nd Lt R M Findlay with his observer Blaiklock.

The squadron could look back on a month of high drama, success and solid achievement tainted by loss, a month in which Belgrave had played a significant role as No 45 emerged as a considerable fighting force despite the handicap of its increasingly obsolescent Strutters. The squadron had destroyed twelve enemy aircraft and claimed a further fifteen driven down out of control. The cost was five aircrew dead, three wounded and three prisoners, one of whom was also injured. About nineteen aircraft were written off, mostly through accidents. Jeff Jefford, who has analysed the results, points out in *The Flying Camels* that, by that time, more Germans were falling to the guns of observers than those of the pilots. It has already been shown that the defensive fire from the observers could be decisive when the Strutters kept in formation. Aggressive pilots of the calibre of Belgrave and Cock, and Lubbock before them, used their forward-firing Vickers to good effect but also gave their observers chances to find a target. Despite some observers becoming aces in their own right, it was inevitably the pilots rather than the rear-seat men who came to be glamourised in tales of aerial combat.

With the arrival of June, Belgrave had been with the squadron six months. It was time for a rest. The authorities had come to recognise the need to give fliers less stressful postings for a period so they could recover from the physical effort and nervous strain of aerial combat. Belgrave had killed and narrowly avoided attempts to kill him. He had seen friends shot out of the sky. He had entered the mess to find that comrades, whether eager newcomers he had barely got to know or veterans – if the term can be applied to men in their early twenties – were missing, never to return. An infantryman might consider the squadron's losses nothing in a war where most of a battalion could be wiped out in minutes. However, as Belgrave knew from his own experience, life in the trenches was not constant attack and counter-attack. There were periods of comparative calm and regular withdrawals for rest in billets behind the lines. Whenever the RFC took to the sky, however, it effectively went looking for trouble by flying east across enemy territory. It was a relentless offensive. An officer needed to be removed from that environment before the pressure evidenced perhaps by snappy remarks or a slight nervous twitch developed into fatally reckless behaviour or complete breakdown. It is not clear how it was decided when the time was right to send a man back to a posting in England. Cock, for instance, was staying on at Ste-Marie-Cappel even though he had arrived in France with the squadron six weeks before Belgrave joined. As Belgrave packed his kit word came through that he had been awarded the Military Cross, officially the squadron's first gallantry award. It would be listed in the *London Gazette* on July 18. Cock was awarded the squadron's second MC, gazetted on July 26. Eglington's MC, for his wing-walking exploits, was not gazetted until August 16. Belgrave's citation read: 'For conspicuous gallantry and devotion to duty. On at least five occasions he successfully engaged and shot down hostile aeroplanes, and has consistently shown great courage and determination to get to the closest range; an invaluable example in a fighting squadron.' The awards were welcome though many felt the squadron had had to wait too long for recognition, given the many outstanding feats of courage since its arrival in France.

Belgrave, the purple and silver ribbon of the MC already sewn on to his tunic, boarded the troop ship home as No 45, without him, entered its bloodiest month of the war. The Allies were switching the emphasis of the infantry effort to Flanders with the broad intention of removing the enemy from the Belgian coast. The first step was to capture the Messines-Wytschaete Ridge to deny the Germans a position from which they could observe preparations for the push. No 45 Squadron, as part of 2nd Brigade, had a vital role to play when the Battle of Messines started on June 7 in an offensive that would lead to the nightmare of Passchendaele. The month had started badly. On June 5 Sergeant Cook and 2/AM Shaw went down in flames, two of five squadron members killed that day in a fight with Albatros scouts over Menin. On June 7 Gwyn Davies, the 23-year-old from Monmouthshire who had got off to such a good start as Belgrave's observer twelve days previously, was lost with his pilot Dobson. Five days later Mountford and Vessey died when their Strutter collided in mid-air with another Sopwith skirting clouds above Ste-Marie-Cappel. That left only Cock out of the original aircrew of No 45 Squadron who had flown to France the previous October. He lasted until July 22 when he was shot down by a pilot of Red Baron Manfred von Richthofen's Jasta 11, a component of the newly formed Flying Circus. Cock, wounded in the ankle and lucky not to go down in flames as petrol spewed from his riddled fuel tank, was taken prisoner. His official tally of victories at the time stood at twelve, though Cock himself considered the true figure to be nineteen for him and his observers, of which he regarded fifteen as certainties. Regardless of whose arithmetic is more accurate, Cock was easily the most successful Strutter pilot of No 45 Squadron or indeed the RFC.

The Squadron had suffered seventeen fatalities by the end of June. Life for Belgrave, meanwhile, was meant to be a whole lot safer as he was posted to squadrons at home. Records show him joining No 81 Squadron on June 7 but by July 23 he is listed with No 37 (Home Defence) Squadron. That unit flew BE12a aircraft from Goldhanger, near the Essex coast, and Sopwith Pups from Stow Maries further inland. It is known that Belgrave flew both types at some stage. Amid wholesale reorganisation of air defences an element of No 37 Squadron was redesignated No 61 (Home Defence) Squadron, based at Rochford, now Southend Airport. From August 7 Belgrave served under No 61, which was part of a defensive ring established round London in response to German air raids. The new commanding officer, Major E R Pretyman, was delighted to have an officer of Belgrave's proven worth.

To most people there is only one Battle of Britain, the crucial struggle of 1940 when the RAF's 'Few' defied the might of the Luftwaffe. However, British BEs, Pups, Camels and Bristols were pitched against Zeppelin airships and Gotha and Giant bombers striking at London and other targets by day and night during the First World War. Over four years 4,830 people were killed and injured by bombing. The figure pales in comparison to the slaughter of the Western Front and perhaps that is why the story of that first air battle over England is largely untold. A Zeppelin scare started well before the war when there were reports of a German airship being flown over Sheerness on October 13 1912. The first raid of wartime came on December 21 1914 when a German floatplane dropped two bombs in the sea off Dover to no effect. Three days later a bomb from another seaplane landed in Dover, leaving a crater in a garden and a few broken windows. The first winter of the war saw other small-scale raids. In May 1915 the Kaiser gave formal authority for attacks on London east of the Tower and Zeppelins steadily exacted a toll of dead, injured and damage to property. Airships may have looked lumbering beasts and were filled with highly-inflammable hydrogen but they could usually outclimb attacking aircraft and proved remarkably difficult to shoot down. Just how vulnerable London was to aerial attack was shown on May 25 1917, Friday of the Whit weekend. It was still daylight when twenty-one twin-engine Gotha bombers crossed the Essex coast and headed for the capital. As luck would have it, clouds forced them to turn south and drop most of their bombs on Folkestone, killing ninety-five people and injuring 195. Not one Gotha was intercepted. The G IV model of the Gotha – the G stood for *Grossflugzeug* or large aeroplane – had a ceiling of nearly 17,000ft, a 78ft wingspan and 260hp Mercedes engines that made it a formidable challenge to contemporary British aircraft.

There was a reluctance to pull back experienced pilots and the best aircraft from the Western Front but amid mounting public consternation over the bombing the War Office approved an up-grading of the Home Defence Group to Brigade status with three Wings. No 61 was one of four day fighter squadrons in Eastern Wing. Belgrave, long frustrated by the limitations of Sopwith's Strutter, was delighted to find himself at the controls of an agile single-seat scout from the same firm, the biplane Pup. The Pup was lacking in power compared to the legendary Camel which was to follow it but No 61's aircraft had the 100hp Monosoupape engine which gave them an edge over Pups equipped with the 80hp Le Rhône.

Belgrave had his first crack at the Gothas on August 12 when eleven of them made a daylight raid on Southend, hardly two miles from No 61's base, killing thirty-three people. Belgrave was airborne at 5.19pm in A6243, one of sixteen of the squadron's Pups sent up. No 61 was virtually the only squadron to engage the enemy that evening. Belgrave and nine other pilots sighted the Gothas as they headed for home, climbing to 14,000ft, lightened of their bomb loads. Belgrave, Captain C A Ridley, Lt L F Hutcheon and 2nd Lt P Thompson kept up the chase for forty or fifty miles, firing from twenty to 270 rounds apiece before their guns jammed. Hutcheon's aircraft B1771 was hit in the engine cowling and lower port wing by a German gunner shooting from the tunnel in the fuselage of his Gotha which allowed him to fire behind and below. Belgrave landed safely after two hours in the air.

He was sent on the trail of Gothas again on the morning of August 22. Belgrave was in A6243, one of eighteen Pups from No 61 seeking ten Gothas which had targeted Margate, Ramsgate and Dover. But none of the Pups was able to engage the enemy and a disappointed Belgrave landed after an hour and a quarter. However, a little bit of history had been made during the attempt to reach the Gothas. 2nd Lt Leonard Lucas of No 50 Squadron in his BE12 'tracker' aircraft transmitted the first air-to-ground wireless message for home defence use. It was one step in the technological race to provide listening, observing and transmission aids in the defence against air attack.

Belgrave was appointed a flight commander on September 1, automatically giving him the rank of temporary Captain. Chasing Gothas was generally somewhat safer than tangling with the Jastas but mishaps could happen as easily at home as in France. Belgrave was fortunate to escape with his life in a flying accident at Rochford on the afternoon of October 6. He was taking up Pup A653 to test its gun when he collided with an Avro. Luckily the crash was at low altitude and he sustained only a black eye and slight concussion when his machine slide-slipped into the ground. The reasons for the accident are unknown as there are no records of blame being apportioned but it seems obvious someone had failed to watch where he was going. By the time Belgrave faced a medical board at Shoeburyness ten days later he had recovered sufficiently to be rated fit for light duties. But he was not considered well enough to take to the air and his flying pay of five shillings (25p) a day was duly stopped. A month after the accident Belgrave made a few flights to see whether altitude had any ill effects after his concussion but found all was well. A medical board on November 20 confirmed that he had made a rapid recovery and suffered no headaches or lack of balance. He was passed fit to resume general service and his flying pay was immediately restored.

By then the Germans had turned to night raids in an attempt to reduce bomber losses. No 61 was better equipped to meet the new threat as they now had the SE5a, one of the best British fighters of the war. The SE5a, a product of the Royal Aircraft Factory, had a 200hp, liquid-cooled Hispano-Suiza or Wolseley Viper V8 engine. This made it less agile, while at the same time more forgiving to the clumsy or uninitiated, than its contemporary the Camel, whose control characteristics were dictated by the large gyroscopic forces of a rotary engine. The early SE5 suffered some minor teething problems but, developed as the SE5a, it was welcomed by pilots as a fine, powerful gun platform with a single Vickers firing through the prop and a Lewis mounted on a Foster rail on the top wing, allowing it to be pulled down for drum changes. The SE5a, usually painted drab olive-green at No 61, could do 126mph at 10,000ft. It could be tricky to land at night, particularly as flashes from the exhaust spoiled the pilot's vision when the engine was throttled back. Dampers on the end of the exhaust pipes solved the problem. Belgrave was flying his SE5a C5302 on the night of February 16/17 1918, hunting four of the huge new German bombers, aptly named Giants, which had targeted Dover and London, killing twelve people. Giants, which dwarfed the Gothas, had six, five or four engines. The four-engined R.IV version encountered by No 61 Squadron had a wingspan of 138ft (the Second World War Lancaster's was 102ft). Seven pilots of No 61 took off in pursuit, Belgrave getting airborne at 10.20pm. About thirty minutes later, attracted by searchlights probing the sky south of the Thames, he encountered R39, one of the Giants, flying south-east very fast at 10,500ft. It and one other Gotha had Maybach 245hp engines, providing a greater range, and so they had reached London while the other two, Mercedes-equipped, examples came no further than Dover. Belgrave fired six long bursts at the monster from about a hundred yards then lost the bomber as he cleared a gun stoppage. He soon found R39 again but abandoned the chase south-east of Maidstone after his gun jammed again. Had he brought down the bomber it would have been a unique achievement – not one Giant fell to the defenders of Britain during the war.

One of Belgrade's comrades in the hunt for Giants that night was Captain C A Lewis in B658. Tall and dashing, Cecil Lewis had been with No 56 Squadron and was on patrol with Ball the evening the latter died. After the war Lewis was a flying instructor, test pilot, a founder of the BBC and author. His 1936 book *Sagittarius Rising* is probably still the classic of First World War flying. He thought Rochford was a 'magnificent aerodrome', handy for dances in Southend and an easy train ride to London when night-flying duties permitted. Lewis also explained how the problem of landing at night was overcome. Flares were made up from chopped-off petrol tins, half-filled with cotton waste and soaked with paraffin. They were positioned on the landing ground in a 'L' shape, the long arm pointing into wind and the short arm marking the limit by which an aircraft should have stopped after landing. The night after the bomber-chasing adventure Belgrave and Lewis were in the air together again. A lone Giant had targeted London, killing twenty-one people and injuring thirty-two. Most of the casualties were at St Pancras railway station and hotel where a stick of eight bombs fell. None of the seven pilots of No 61 sent up that night found the Giant. Belgrave landed back at Rochford shortly before midnight. Lewis also returned safely after being forced to avoid what would now be termed friendly fire. His SE5a collected some holes when an aircraft flying west over Benfleet started shooting. Assuming it could not be the enemy, Lewis spun away. Sometimes night fighters were held in searchlights and fired on by anti-aircraft guns. The excuse from the gunners was that two fighters could sound like one Gotha. Towards the end of Belgrave's time with No 61, one of the pilots who had flown with him on that last mission was killed in a night accident. Captain Henry

Stroud in his SE5a was in a mid-air collision with Captain Alexander Kynoch of No 37 Squadron flying a BE12. Kynoch also died as both aircraft crashed on farmland at Rawreth, Essex. It happened on the night of March 7/8 while both men were seeking German raiders. The pilots had taken off within minutes of each other, Stroud from Rochford and Kynoch from Goldhanger.

German bomber raids on England ended in May though by April Belgrave had gone. He was needed back on the Western Front. The Kaiser had made his last throw of the dice with a huge spring offensive. The outcome of the war was in the balance and scout squadrons were desperate for officers of Belgrave's experience.

# CHAPTER FIVE

# A TOPPING GOOD FELLOW

THE Red Baron was dead. Rittmeister Manfred Freiherr von Richthofen had fallen fatally into the simple trap that he always warned his men to avoid. Well overdue a rest, the German ace of aces had become so fixated on trying to make Lt Wilfred 'Wop' May's Sopwith Camel his eighty-first victory that he broke his own cardinal rule by chasing the British aeroplane low over Allied-held territory. Canadian Captain Roy Brown would enter legend as the man who dived to May's rescue but latest research indicates that the Baron was killed by a single bullet from an Australian machine-gunner on the ground. Richthofen crashed to his death on the Morlancourt Ridge above the River Somme on April 21 1918. Word of the Baron's demise spread rapidly through the aerodromes of the Royal Air Force, which had been formed from the Royal Flying Corps and Royal Naval Air Service at the beginning of that month. James Belgrave, who had joined No 60 Squadron only two days before the Baron's demise, heard the news in the tented village serving as the squadron's base outside the lonely hamlet of Boffles, about ten miles north-west of Doullens. The reaction there was probably typical. Satisfaction that the fabled red triplane would claim no more Allied lives was tempered by respect for a valiant fallen foe, an emotion perhaps surprising so late in the war when any lingering notions of chivalry might have vanished beneath the mud of Passchendaele.

As the British and Australians buried Richthofen with full military honours at the village of Bertangles some twenty miles south of Boffles Belgrave was settling into his new posting. No 60 was a scout unit equipped with the SE5a with which Belgrave was familiar from his time on home defence. This was the squadron where Albert Ball had amassed more than thirty victories in 1916 during five intense weeks of lone forays in his personal little Nieuport. Canadian ace Billy Bishop was also a member of No 60 when he launched an audacious solo, low-level attack on a German airfield on June 2 1917. He machine-gunned parked aircraft, shot down one Albatros as it took off to challenge him, forced another to crash, then did battle with two more Germans, shooting down one before limping home, out of ammunition and with his Nieuport's fuselage and wings riddled by small-arms fire from the ground. The astonishing feat earned Bishop the Victoria Cross. Some air historians doubt Bishop's version of events, pointing out that, of the fifty-one VCs won by airmen in two world wars, his is unique in being based on personal evidence only, unsupported by witnesses from either side. Bishop's supporters are vehement in their protests against any suggestion that their hero was a conman.

The squadron had been at Boffles only one week when Belgrave arrived. The Germans, determined to break through to the Atlantic coast to end the war before the full might of American reinforcements could be thrown against them, had launched their massive push on March 21. The following day No 60 Squadron moved from Bailleul to the Somme front where it was sorely needed to play a part in stemming the tide with offensive patrols and low-level sorties. Its first base in its new sector was Bellevue, six miles east of Doullens, under 13th Wing of 3rd Brigade. Only four days later the squadron was on the move again, pulling back to Fienvillers, six miles south-west of Doullens, in the face of the enemy advance. The Germans had gained some forty miles and were threatening Amiens. In little more than a week they had regained most of the territory which the British had taken six months of terrible fighting to win in 1916. The Allies withdrew to what was termed the Amiens Defence Line. The Front was thus straightened and reduced, making a denser, more co-ordinated defence possible. No 60 found Fienvillers in chaos, overcrowded as it was with other squadrons and suffering the effects of recent German bombing. The disruption caused to communications by the retreat added to the confusion. Despite the handicaps the squadron put in some fine work during this period with patrols and low-level bombing. Eight enemy aircraft were downed by one patrol alone. No 60 had been at Fienvillers barely three weeks when the move to Boffles was ordered. Belgrave joined a squadron whose tenders were clapped out and whose accumulated treasures had vanished. Bronze figures and silver basins bought on trips into towns, pictures, decanters, souvenirs and trophies such as German sign boards and shell cases; all had been lost or left behind. The accommodation at Boffles, which was to remain the squadron's home for five months, was poor. There were bell tents, a few Nissen huts and some delapidated wooden buildings. Amid the administrative confusion, pay had fallen into arrears and there was little cash about, not that there was much time or opportunity to spend it. Belgrave had gone to No 60 to take over command of B Flight, keeping his rank of Captain. The squadron CO was Barry Moore, who knew him from Rochford. While there Moore had flown with No 198 Depot Squadron and had also been with No 28 Training Squadron at Castle Bromwich. Before the RFC and RAF, he was with the Royal Warwicks, the regiment in which Belgrave's brother Charles served. Belgrave was pleased to be back in France for another crack at the enemy, this time properly equipped for the job with the SE5a. Moore assured him there would be plenty to do. The German push was running out of impetus by the end of April but there was much hard fighting ahead. Although the Allies were regaining air superiority the Germans were concentrating their best pilots and aircraft on the Amiens front, where No 60 Squadron operated. Both sides were putting up formations much larger than those of Belgrave's time at Ste-Marie-Cappel.

When Belgrave arrived at Boffles No 60 Squadron usually had about twenty pilots available for flying after leave, sickness and training demands were accounted for. Squadrons had three flights, A, B and C, with six pilots each, though later in the war the establishment was increased slightly. Despite his experience Belgrave was held back from crossing the lines until he had settled in and become familiar with the terrain. He had to content himself with flying a new machine from the depot and putting in the odd practice or test flight. In any case, the weather had been poor and the squadron had met little opposition from enemy fliers for a couple of weeks. However, on May 2 Belgrave found action when he flew to take a look at the lines in B151, an SE5a built by Martinsyde, sub-contractors working at Brooklands, and equipped with the French version of the Hispano-Suiza engine. He was at 14,000ft while south-west of Arras when, attracted by British Archie bursting above him, he saw a two-seater, probably an Albatros, 2,000ft higher. Belgrave later reported: 'I climbed after him and when

NE of Arras got within two hundred yards of the EA slightly below him. As I was not overhauling him fast, I opened fire but after a short burst both guns stopped. Before I could clear the stoppages the EA drew away.' Moore was not sympathetic about the gun jams. He noted on Belgrave's combat report: 'The Vickers gun stoppage was caused by the pilot not loading correctly, failing to pull the cocking handle properly.' The over-wing Lewis gun was defective and Moore called for a report on the reason for its failure. Not surprisingly, Belgrave's encounter with the German machine was rated indecisive. It was not the most auspicious of starts but Belgrave was entering the busiest and most successful period of his flying career.

Next day thirteen of the squadron's aircraft took to the air at midday, with Belgrave leading his flight. Fellow Military Cross holder Captain Owen Scholte led C Flight, of which he had just taken command. Scholte was the 24-year-old son of a Viennese tailor who had emigrated to London to work. He became a despatch rider on the outbreak of war, before being commissioned in the Bedfordshire Regiment. Scholte transferred to the RFC in 1915 and had claimed six victories flying Bristol Fighters with No 48 Squadron by the time he arrived at No 60 Squadron via a spell at home. Neither Belgrave nor Scholte were to add to their tally that day. No enemy aircraft was seen during the two-hour patrol though two of the pilots reported seeing an explosion and large fires on the ground. May 4 was as quiet with Belgrave and Scholte going up in the afternoon with two more pilots to practise for a little over an hour. The next few days were quiet thanks to low cloud and mist. On May 8 Belgrave, having taken another machine up for a test flight in the morning, was back in B151 after lunch for an offensive patrol. Scholte and seven other pilots took off with him at 1pm. Lt Alfred Saunders had to turn back after forty-five minutes with a faulty magneto and the others ran into a storm just before reaching the lines at 12,000ft. Through the clouds below Belgrave saw an Albatros two-seater and dived after it. As he cleared the cloud he was still a hundred yards from the aircraft, which was heading west. As soon as Belgrave fired a short burst the German sought cover by diving into another cloud layer. Ignoring the perils of flying virtually blind in cloud, Belgrave dropped into the layer only to find that when he emerged the German had vanished. Undeterred, Belgrave was in the air again that evening, taking two other pilots on a roving commission in the hope of finding the enemy. But they saw nothing on a flight lasting 2hrs 20mins. Belgrave went up in B155 on another roving commission on the afternoon of May 9. He spotted three enemy two-seaters at 13,000ft but was unable to engage them. Determined to salvage something from the day, he was airborne again at 5.40pm, less than two hours after landing. This time Scholte in C1056 went with him and a little after an hour in the air the pair saw some SE5s scrapping with Albatros scouts at 12,000ft east of Villers-Brettoneux. Belgrave said in his combat report: 'I flew over to the fight and saw one EA to the north of the SEs. I attacked this machine and fired a long burst from my Lewis gun, upon which the EA dived east through a layer of clouds.' Belgrave could find an enemy and engage him but, to his frustration, closing for the kill was proving a little harder.

He tangled with the enemy again the following afternoon. Although a decisive victory still eluded him, he was able at least to help Lt Saunders to success. Belgrave was leading nine SE5s patrolling over enemy territory between Bapaume and Peronne at 13,000ft. The visibility was reasonable and the British fliers saw plumes of black smoke billowing from what looked like a petrol dump ablaze at Harbonnieres. By 5.30pm the formation was near Albert when Belgrave spotted about nine Pfalz DIII scouts off to the east and slightly higher than the SE5s. The Pfalz, a sturdy, Mercedes-powered biplane, had twin Spandau machine-guns but was not as fast as the SE5a. Belgrave reported: 'I climbed to the attack and opened fire at one EA at about 150 yards. This machine dived past me and Lt Saunders attacked it. I then got under the tail of another EA and opened fire with both guns at about fifty yards' range and apparently did good shooting.' Lt Gordon Duncan, a 19-year-old Scot, saw the second German tip into a spin then enter a vertical dive; Belgrave was too busy fixing a gun stoppage to watch what happened. Then he and Duncan turned to chase off the remaining Germans, losing any chance of seeing whether the Pfalz hit the ground. Saunders, however, had finished off the first Pfalz attacked by Belgrave. Flying C5450, he managed a close burst as the white machine passed under him. He got on to the German's tail and gave him a longer burst. Saunders noted tersely: 'The EA turned over and over forwards completely out of control. My Lewis gun striker pin broke and I pulled out.' Lt R Kirkpatrick saw the burning wreck. For Saunders, who had been with No 60 since the previous October, it was the first of an eventual twelve victories and it would not be the last time that he partnered Belgrave in destroying enemy aircraft. 'Pat' Saunders, a 30-year-old Dubliner, had been with the Royal Field Artillery in the Darndanelles before transferring to the RFC. All the SE5s returned to Boffles safely, apart from C5499 flown by 20-year-old Welshman Lt Glyn Lewis, who had to make a forced landing at No 59 Squadron's airfield at Fienvillers after his engine's oil pressure faded. All in all, a good day for the squadron. Belgrave commented that, on this occasion, the Germans had shown very little inclination to fight, turning east as soon as the SE5s moved in. It is perhaps worth noting at this stage that, although it was May, Belgrave and his comrades were operating, and fighting, in temperatures of well below zero. Heavy flying gear helped but the thin air at altitudes often well in excess of two miles deprived the fliers of precious oxygen with no artificial supply to offset the debilitating effects. Coupled with the nervous tension, it meant a two-hour patrol was incredibly taxing mentally and physically.

The next few days were unfruitful. On May 13 Belgrave and Scholte, with eight other pilots, took off for a patrol at 7am. Hampered by poor visibility and clouds at 6,000ft, they returned after two hours without having seen any enemy aircraft. The following day was even more of a dud. Belgrave started by taking B151 for a twenty-minute practice flight. At 2.30pm he swapped to C5439 for a two-hour patrol, leading four other aircraft. He saw nothing and the flight turned to a fiasco. Saunders had to land at No 5 Squadron's airfield at Le Hameau, nearly out of fuel. Lewis touched down at nearby Serny with the same problem. Kirkpatrick's engine failed and he pranged as he made a forced landing at Tangry. Only Duncan flew back with Belgrave to Boffles without mishap.

Wednesday May 15 dawned fine and German aircraft were plentiful. It was a good day for No 60 to go hunting and an excellent chance for Belgrave to open his scoring with the squadron. Flying B151 again, he was leading his patrol east of Arras when at 11.45am he saw two Rumpler two-seaters heading west towards the lines. They were thousands of feet higher than the British machines, which were at 15,000ft. Belgrave at once started climbing and followed the Germans along a course of roughly Doullens-Hesdin-Lens. It was a long haul and when Belgrave and Saunders, the pilots who got closest, opened fire both their Lewis guns jammed. By now the Germans were almost at 21,000ft, about the ceiling for an SE5a. Belgrave and his comrades had to resort to zooming, that is going into a shallow dive to pick up speed before pulling up sharply to claw some height. Belgrave said in his combat report: 'I got within fifty feet at one period but could only fire a very short burst before stalling, though I must have obtained hits.' The outcome was rated indecisive. However, Scholte, in C5385, scored his first victory since joining the squadron, and his seventh overall, when he shot down one of the Rumplers in flames. He fired several bursts from both guns. The enemy machine immediately went east, followed by Scholte firing the remainder of the Lewis drum at close range into it. The Rumpler caught fire and crashed north-east of a small wood near Lamotte. The whole encounter had taken about an hour. It was later found that Belgrave's Lewis gun had failed because of a broken extractor, which left an empty cartridge case in the chamber. On Saunders' weapon the bolt had broken.

Belgrave at last achieved success that evening when he was leading a twelve-aircraft formation and, as if to make up for lost time, he scored a double victory. Again, the enemy aircraft were first encountered east of Arras. At 7.45pm Belgrave, flying at 15,000ft in C1056, saw eighteen brightly-coloured Albatros DV scouts in three groups slightly above the British machines. Despite the odds, he immediately turned to meet them. 'I climbed and attacked from out of the sun,' he reported. 'The EA mostly dived from us, but I was able to catch up a purple machine, and dived on its nose. He then dived very steeply but I was able to do an "Immelmann" on to his tail and fired a burst from both guns at less than fifty yards' range. The EA went down in a corkscrew spin and I saw him crash south of the Arras-Cambrai road.' In less than five minutes Belgrave had climbed and seen another Albatros to the east. It had throttled back and was rocking from side to side as if damaged. Belgrave said: 'I came up under his tail and fired a burst from my Lewis gun at close range. The EA then rolled over and went down in a wide spiral spin, apparently out of control, but I lost sight of him when at low altitude.' Lt Meredith Davies, a Welsh pilot with the squadron for only a few weeks, saw the Albatros spinning down near Croisilles and accounted for another German himself. He reported: 'I attacked a straggler who promptly dived away. I followed him down for about 4,000ft, firing short bursts with both guns. I saw my tracers entering the machine. I then pulled out as there were other EA above me unoccupied. When I last saw him he was diving vertically. I saw one machine spinning down above me and into the sun.' Davies's victim burst into flames, with 19-year-old 2nd Lt Frederick Clark also firing about a hundred rounds into the Albatros before pulling out. Belgrave was again left unimpressed by the Germans' fighting spirit. 'The EA, though greatly outnumbering us, showed very little fight and eventually all went eastwards,' he noted.

The 'Immelmann' that Belgrave used to close on his first Albatros was a turn said to have been invented by Max Immelmann earlier in the war, although the renowned German ace never made mention of it himself. Different descriptions have been attempted of the manouevre, executed by a pilot to give himself a second chance after he had dived and overshot while trying to shoot down an enemy aircraft. By Belgrave's time the technique seemed to involve the attacker going into a steep climb after the initial swoop then, as his machine was about to stall, kicking the rudder to enter a steep turning dive. With any luck, that would put him back on his opponent's tail. It certainly worked for Belgrave. The Germans' reluctance to fight that evening meant that the British patrol was involved in only about eight individual engagements. The only 'casualties' on the British side were Kirkpatrick, who again crashed on landing, though not seriously, Lt C R Henderson, who made a forced landing at No 57 Squadron with air pressure trouble, and Lewis, who landed at No 41 Squadron, short of petrol. By the time he refuelled it was too dark to fly to Boffles. Saunders, too, had been on the patrol as had one of the squadron's most intriguing characters, 2nd Lt Alex Beck. An Anglo-Argentinian, Beck had been at school in England at the outbreak of war. He joined the RFC and was posted to No 60 Squadron in July 1917. He was sent home from France the following month when his parents informed the authorities he was under age. By then he had already flown thirteen sorties over the lines. Undeterred, Beck returned to the squadron in March 1918 as soon as he was old enough.

Belgrave was in the air again at 7.30am next day. In B151, he was leading his patrol at 10,000ft over the squadon's normal patch of east of Arras when at 8.40am he saw two German aircraft well below. The SE5s dived to the attack and opened fire. One of the enemy aircraft, an LVG two-seater reconnaissance machine, dived under Belgrave. He reported: 'I then turned on his tail and fired a burst from both guns at very close range (from fifty to twenty yards). I then had to pull out to avoid colliding. When I again dived I overshot the EA very quickly, from which I think his engine had been hit. I fired another burst and both my guns stopped but I followed the EA, who was gliding very unsteadily and swinging from side to side, until I was at 4,000ft. I then saw the EA go down and land in a field north-east of Arras, apparently without crashing.' The other LVG fell moments later to the guns of Lt John Griffith in D3503 and Lt Herbert Hegarty in B190. The German machine went into a vertical dive and crashed in flames near Fampoux. For Griffith, a 19-year-old American from Seattle, it was his fifth confirmed victory; for Hegarty his sixth. By that time pilots from the United States Air Service were filtering their way into RAF squadrons in France but it appears that Griffith had joined the RFC of his own accord and had been with No 60 since 1917.

By 9.20am Belgrave was back on the ground. It had been a good morning's work but his appetite for action remained far from sated. By 3pm B151 had been readied for another patrol. Belgrave led a twelve-aircraft formation, soon reduced to eleven when Henderson dropped out with instrument trouble. The flight, deep into enemy territory, brought Belgrave the ninth victory of his career, not counting that morning's 'forced to land' success. It also gave him the opportunity to help Saunders to another victory. It was 4.15pm when the patrol found nine Albatros scouts at 17,000ft above Bapaume. The enemy machines were heading north-west and Belgrave manoeuvred to get into the sun before launching an attack. Belgrave's combat report continued the story: 'I opened fire at one EA who dived vertically then started spinning. Lt Saunders followed him down and engaged him later. I was at about 11,000ft and I saw an EA just below me and to the south. I dived on this machine and fired both guns into him at about fifty yards' range. After a long burst the EA dived vertically, emitting black smoke. Just then another EA passed me and went after another SE5. I then dived after the EA and opened fire at long range (about two hundred yards). The EA, who was firing smoke tracer, turned off the SE5's tail. I followed him down to about 4,000ft firing several bursts, but the EA outdived me and turned east. As there were two other Albatros scouts above me and to the east I climbed up and joined three other SE5s. The flight took place between Bapaume and Albert.' Saunders confirmed that he had dived headlong after the first Albatros, flashing past two other SE5s who were scrapping with another German. The Albatros continued spinning down to 3,000ft before flattening out and scurrying east to safety. Saunders then positioned himself on the sun side of the German scouts, hoping his intended prey would return to the fray, which he did. The German, evidently blinded by the sun, failed to see Saunders' head-on attack in C5450 until too late. 'I gave him a complete drum of Lewis and over hundred rounds of Vickers at very close range,' said Saunders. 'The EA dived directly under me into the ground and crashed badly. I flew twice round the spot to locate same.' The German, Saunders' second confirmed victory, had hit the ground at Beaulencourt, south of Bapaume. Saunders climbed back towards the action and made another head-on attack on an Albatros at about 6,000ft. But the striking pin of his Lewis had broken and the German made good his escape by tipping into a spin before pulling out and flying east. Saunders headed home.

Belgrave's three scraps were officially noted as indecisive. Squadron CO Major Moore noted on Belgrave's combat report: 'I should like confirmation of these from AA, especially the second combat as Captain Belgrave states that the smoke in question was much more than exhaust.' That fight is now usually credited to Belgrave as a victory in the 'out of control' category.

The success had come at a price. Early in the flight 2nd Lt Herbert Proctor had been shot down and killed in D3912. Birmingham-born Proctor had flown under Belgrave's leadership four times before, including the previous day. He was 19. His was the squadron's first death in action since Belgrave joined and it is believed he was the eighteenth victim of 27-year-old Leutnant Fritz Rumey, of the highly successful Jasta 5. Rumey would survive long enough to win the Pour le Mérite and push his score to forty-five before dying in a mid-air collision with an SE5a of No 32 Squadron in September. It is perhaps worth explaining here that an SE5a pilot trying to shoot down a foe would usually use his Lewis and Vickers guns simultaneously for maximum concentrated firepower. The triggers for both weapons were closely aligned on the aircraft's control column so a single thumb would operate both. The guns could be operated individually if wished. The pilot aimed using a two-inch Aldis optical sight and a ring-and-bead sight.

Belgrave was up looking for action again early on the morning of May 17. He was with Saunders and Lewis when at 5am they caught a Rumpler two-seater unawares east of Albert. The German only spotted them only as they tried to cut off his line of retreat and he went into a dive. Belgrave in B151, Saunders in C5450 and Lewis in B8398 dived from 4,000ft, all firing at the enemy machine. Belgrave reported: 'I myself fired a long burst from both guns into the EA at between one and two hundred yards' range and both the pilots in my formation saw my tracer going into and all around the EA fuselage.' However, Belgrave was unable to finish off the Rumpler for certain as both his guns had stoppages. By the time he rectified the problems he had lost sight of the German. Saunders and Lewis followed the Rumpler down to a few hundred feet and it apparently landed in or near a valley south of Contalmaison. Later that morning Lt W J A 'Art' Duncan was on a lone patrol in C9536 when he saw fifteen German aircraft attacking an RE8 near Bapaume. Contemptuous of the odds, he dived in and shot the wing off one Albatros DV as it disappeared through the clouds. It was his ninth victory. He created such confusion among the rest of the Germans, driving down two of them, that the RE8 was able to escape. Duncan, a 26-year-old Canadian from Sault Ste Marie, Ontario, who had joined the RFC in 1916, was awarded a bar to his MC for his action. He had been acting CO of A Flight while

Captain W Copeland was in England testing new scouts. This took longer than expected so Duncan was promoted Captain and took command of the flight. The evening of Duncan's triumph Belgrave led a patrol on a two-hour flight but there was to be no repeat of the success. He brought his flight home without having seen an enemy aircraft.

Next morning, however, Belgrave's persistence was rewarded with his tenth and eleventh victories. It was a fine day and, though enemy activity in the sky was limited, Belgrave found plenty of action. In B151, he took off with Griffith and Saunders at 10.25am but Griffith was forced to return after only ten minutes with engine trouble. At 11.15am Belgrave and Lewis in B8419 were east of Albert at 16,000ft when they saw a DFW two-seater. Belgrave said in his combat report: 'I dived from the south-east and when at about a hundred yards, opened fire. When close on his tail I did an "Immelmann" turn to lose distance and then dived again, putting in a long burst. The EA stalled and I then lost sight of him as I was feeling the effects of the dive. Lt Lewis, however, saw the EA falling out of control.' Within fifteen minutes Belgrave found an Albatros scout in the same area. His report continued: 'I again attacked from the sun diving and then zooming up at him. He at once dived and we fought at close range for several thousand feet. The EA then spun and I followed him down. At about 8,000 feet he came out of the spin and I again dived at him. He then dived vertically and crashed near a wood, near Carnoy.' Belgrave and Lewis climbed and headed back towards Allied territory. 'I had only one machine with me so I kept near our lines,' said Belgrave. 'I saw a formation of seven Albatros scouts east of Albert and getting to the south-west dived at a straggler, but he dived away. I altogether made three attacks on this formation, but apparently without obtaining results. This formation would not fight and withdrew to the east whenever I dived.'

The report is evidence of the way Belgrave, relentlessly aggressive in the attack, rarely let his hunger for results cloud his judgment and lead him and comrades into recklessness and possible traps over enemy territory. In his brief time with the squadron he had matured impressively to become its finest patrol leader. In particular his performance over the previous four days so stirred Major Moore that he acted to seek official recognition for Belgrave. That evening he wrote to 13th Wing headquarters urging the staff to consider 'such award as you deem fit'. Moore outlined the recent achievements and added this testimonial: 'Captain Belgrave as a patrol leader is magnificent, possessing the greatest initiative and showing utter fearlessness. His influence on the squadron's morale is extremely great. He has only been with the squadron four weeks and during that time has partaken in many other fights, and has probably crashed several other EA but owing to lack of information and his own modesty he has not claimed them.'

Belgrave had no intention of resting on his laurels. On May 19 he took off at 9am, leading a twelve-aircraft formation. At 10am he saw three enemy two-seaters flying low and put C9536 into a dive from 12,000ft. Before he could engage the aircraft he found himself close to a German kite balloon and took the opportunity to attack it instead. He put several long bursts into it at close range without the slightest effect. It might be thought that observation balloons with a vulnerable observer dangling in a basket beneath made easy targets. However, it proved difficult to destroy them using the ordinary ammunition and tracer with which Belgrave's guns were loaded that day. Pilots on balloon-busting missions usually used Buckingham ammunition, phosphorus-filled incendiary bullets named after the Coventry engineer who developed them. Even then balloons were a risky proposition as anti-aircraft guns were positioned to protect them. Belgrave would probably have had more success with the two-seaters; Captain Scholte did. In C5385 he attacked one of the Hannover CL fighter-reconnaisance machines from underneath. It burst into flames and broke up in the air east of Arras. Later in the patrol Belgrave and Lt Robert Whitney chased five Albatros Scouts but they flew east. Perhaps in frustration as much as hope, Belgrave opened fire at the nearest German from five hundred yards. It dived away to the east, as did another he aimed at from long range. An idea of how unreliable aircraft of the era were can be seen from the fact that five of the pilots who took off that morning had to cut short their flight through technical problems. Hegarty returned to Boffles with falling oil pressure followed by Lt E R Ortner, whose carburettor was playing up. Davies and Saunders had their propellers burst after the encounter with the Germans. Both made successful forced landings at Bellevue accompanied by 2nd Lt Clark. Belgrave's B151 had been in the workshop that morning for work on its engine. It proved satisfactory during a ten-minute test flight in the afternoon and Belgrave led an eight-aircraft patrol in B151 that evening. A German two-seater was seen over Morlancourt but was not engaged. Saunders managed to crash on landing when the patrol returned to Boffles at 8.45pm. Belgrave again drew a blank the following day. He led a two-hour morning patrol of seven aircraft, two of which had to head home with technical problems after an hour.

No enemy machines were encountered. A ninety-minute roving commission in the evening was similarly unproductive. One consolation for Belgrave was that he was able to acquaint himself with the new SE5a that was to be his usual machine in place of B151. D5988 had just arrived from the depot and Belgrave took it up for a fifteen-minute test flight in the afternoon. The Vickers-built machine, with the same French-built version of the Hispano-Suiza as B151, had a fresh coat of matt brown paint and No 60 Squadron's two vertical white bands had been applied round the fuselage just ahead of the tail. The identifying letter N was painted further forward. Belgrave had to wait only until the following morning to give D5988 its blooding.

He was in the air at 7.30am with eight other pilots and an hour later they were in action near Courcelette. Belgrave was intending to have a go at a nearby kite balloon when he saw an LVG, which was slightly above him at 6,000ft and climbing into position to attack. Four Albatros scouts then dived on the British formation from out of the sun. Leaving his comrades to deal with them, Belgrave got under the LVG and opened fire. 'When I was within a hundred yards of the EA he dived steeply and I continued firing until my Lewis drum was expended,' he reported. 'The EA went down out of control with his nose well down in a wide irregular spiral. I last saw him about 1,000ft over Courcelette and then lost him owing to very bad visibilty. A short time afterwards I saw something burning on the ground below where I had last seen the EA.' It was his twelfth victory. The German scouts had been intent on diving on Belgrave but were driven off by the other SE5s and a Camel that arrived on the scene. For some reason Belgrave was alone when a little while later four German scouts, possibly the ones from the previous encounter, came at him from the north-east over Albert. He was by then at 11,000ft and the enemy aircraft were slightly below him, in line with one slightly ahead. Belgrave reported: 'I waited until the front scout was within three or four hundred yards of my tail and then did a half roll and attacked him from directly ahead. We both fired at each other for a short time then the EA turned east and dived away vertically. The other three EA then circled round and lost formation but would not attack.' Aggression tempered by cool awareness had again paid off for Belgrave. Lewis, meanwhile, only just made it back to Boffles in an SE5a with its engine bearer, propellor and left bottom wing badly shot through. The damage was beyond the resources of the fitters at Boffles and the stricken machine was later flown gingerly to the depot and replaced. It was not Glyn Lewis's day. He joined Belgrave's flight again in the evening for an offensive patrol only to make a forced landing at St Pol after an hour when the air pressure pump pipe broke on his stand-in SE5a. Belgrave and the others saw eight Pfalz scouts and eight more enemy machines at 14,000ft between Bapaume and Peronne but the sighting came to nothing.

The morning of May 22 saw Belgrave and Saunders continuing their enthusiastic partnership in opposition to the German air service. Lewis and Gordon Duncan were the other B Flight members who joined them on an offensive patrol. At 11.45am Belgrave saw a DFW north of Bapaume. He pushed D5988 into a dive to attack but the German two-seater was very low and Belgrave was unable to get to close quarters. He saw another DFW over Bapaume at about 7,000ft and opened fire from two hundred yards. His Vickers jammed after a single burst and before he could cure the problem the enemy aircraft got away. Saunders also fired on the enemy machines but apparently to no avail. The two officers had better luck early next morning, sharing a victory after tangling with six Albatros scouts. However, Saunders came perilously close to getting shot down himself until Belgrave helped extricate him from trouble. It had started out as a three-aircraft patrol but Gordon Duncan, flying Belgrave's old machine B151, had to turn back fifteen minutes after the 4.30am take-off when his engine seized. At 5.50am, with the weather fine, Belgrave and Saunders found a DFW over Bapaume and attacked but were unable to get close. They fired from several hundred yards' range and the German vanished off to the east unharmed. Later the British pair saw the Albatros scouts several miles into German territory. They headed towards the enemy aircraft but were unable to climb to their height. Belgrave and Saunders headed west, luring the Germans into giving chase and diving to their own level. However, as the SE5s reached the British lines at about 9,000ft the German pilots peeled off and dived further to investigate black bursts of anti-aircraft fire south of Albert. It gave Belgrave the chance he needed. Now higher than the Germans, he dived to put D5988 on to the tail of the lowest, yellow Albatros, which twisted east then west in a vain bid to shake him off. Belgrave fired both guns from just fifteen feet away, so close that the two aircraft almost collided. He said: 'I actually saw bullets hitting the fuselage and pilot and suddenly he fell back and the machine fell over to the right. I dived under the tail, missing his undercarriage by a few feet.' Saunders, in B137, had dived further into Hunland, ready to cut off the German scout if it tried to escape east. He reported: 'As Captain Belgrave pulled out the Albatros fell out sideways and I got a very close burst directly on to his top planes.

Albatros continued straight dive to the ground and crashed.' As the German plunged to earth near Fricourt, east of Albert, his five comrades hurtled down on Saunders, firing for all their worth. They might have succeeded in exacting revenge if it had not been for desperate evasive tactics by Saunders and timely intervention by Belgrave. Saunders said: 'I went vertically towards the ground zigzagging and pulled out a hundred feet above the ground between Aveluy and Albert. EA followed me close to lines but retired when Captain Belgrave returned to my assistance.' Belgrave confirmed: 'As soon as I opened fire they retired east.'

The two were back at Boffles at 6.30am to celebrate the victory, Belgrave's thirteenth and Saunders' third. It rained throughout the following day, giving the squadron a respite from combat. Visibility was rotten on May 25 and Belgrave found no aircraft on an offensive patrol despite nearly emptying D5988's fuel tank by staying airborne from 9 to 11.15am. Saunders had already had to make a forced landing at No 23 Squadron's aerodrome at Bertangles when the interrupter gear on B137 came off and his propellor broke. To complete the catalogue of mishaps, Gordon Duncan had to land away when C9498 ran short of petrol and Lewis returned to Boffles early with magneto trouble. The next day was another dud with cloud and bad visibility keeping the squadron grounded.

Belgrave was back in his old B151 on the evening of May 27 to put in a long solo sortie over enemy territory but he saw nothing. There was considerably more action to the south. German forces launched a surprise attack along the Aisne front with the aim of drawing Allied reserves away from northern sectors, where the final push was intended to finish off the British Army. The Aisne offensive was so successful, however, that it ran on to the River Marne and threatened Paris. US troops, pouring into France in ever increasing numbers, were pushed in to plug the gap. The RAF still had much to do.

Next day Belgrave was in the air at 4.30am with Saunders, Lewis and Gordon Duncan and forty minutes later he had pushed his victory score to fourteen. At 9,000ft above Albert he saw an LVG two-seater approaching the lines. When it was over Aveluy Wood it turned south-east. Belgrave positioned D5988 under the German aircraft's tail and gave it two bursts from 150 yards. The LVG burst into flames and broke up. A British anti-aircraft battery confirmed its destruction as pieces fell to earth south of Albert. The crew, Leutnants A Schroedter and R E Wittler, of Flieger Abteilung Artillerie (artillery spotting unit) 224, died. Belgrave's aircraft had received hits during his attack but he was able to return to Boffles safely. Saunders had to land at Bellevue when an oil lead on D3966 broke. That evening Belgrave took up C1056 to seek more potential targets but returned after forty-five minutes without having seen anything. A new officer, 2nd Lt John Macvicker, had turned up during the day. Macvicker, from Somerset, was on home defence duties before being sent to France and Belgrave knew him from Rochford. Macvicker was posted to No 60 Squadron after just three days with No 56 Squadron. The rapid nature of the move was perhaps down to some administrative quirk because his arrival coincided with Captain Copeland and Lt Ortner being sent to No 56 from Boffles. Belgrave put Macvicker in B151 next morning and escorted him in D5988 to show him the area. Whether by design or through some technical problem, the pair touched down at No 19 Squadron's aerodrome at Savy forty minutes later. They did not set off home for nearly six hours and it is possible Belgrave used the visit as an opportunity to try out one of No 19's Sopwith Dolphins. It was back to normal business on May 30 with Belgrave leading a two-hour evening offensive patrol with Saunders, Scholte and five other pilots. Despite the good visibility, only one German was seen and he was not engaged. Canadian Lt K Campbell smashed the undercarriage and bottom wings of D328 when he had to put down at No 15 Squadron's airfield with air pressure problems. It was a disappointing end to an already blighted day. New arrival Lt John Headlam, of A Flight, was putting in some firing practice on the aerodrome target when the wings of C5381 collapsed. The aircraft dived into the ground and 19-year-old Headlam, of Whitby, Yorks, was killed. With the weather remaining fine, Belgrave was in the air again at 10am on May 31, leading a twelve-aircraft deep offensive patrol. He spotted seven Albatros scouts and an unidentified two-seater at Villers-Cagnicourt, south-east of Arras, and led an attack from 13,000ft but the outnumbered Germans were reluctant to fight. Belgrave and one other pilot fired from 150 yards, apparently without result, as the enemy headed eastwards. Another two-hour patrol that evening brought Belgrave no better luck. No Germans were in evidence and Lewis crashed near Fienvillers ten minutes after take-off when an oil spindle broke. At least he was unhurt.

Belgrave was told early in June that he had been awarded a bar to his Military Cross, in line with Moore's recommendation. The citation read: 'For conspicuous gallantry and devotion to duty whilst leading offensive patrols. In four days he destroyed two enemy machines and drove down two others. The odds were heavy against him, and he did magnificent work.' Belgrave sewed the silver rosette, denoting the bar, on to the ribbon of his MC. The award was popular with fellow officers and the men for Belgrave – 'Jim' or 'Jimmy' to those closest to him – had shown himself to be as superb a leader on the ground as in the air. Moore even left him in command of the squadron while away temporarily. One of Belgrave's pilots – unfortunately it is not known which one – wrote a letter home: 'Belgrave has been doing awfully well, he has got eight or nine Huns and has got a bar to his MC. He is a topping good fellow and I am awfully lucky to be with him.' It seemed only fair that Belgrave's still temporary rank of Captain should become permanent and Moore again wrote to Wing, urging just that. He said: 'This officer has since joining my squadron proved himself to be a fine leader and organiser and is a highly efficient officer, in all respects. His example has imbued a fine offensive spirit in the officers in his flight. I cannot speak too highly of his work. I recommend him very strongly for promotion to substantive rank of Captain.'

By this time the moment of crisis for the Allies had passed and the situation was improving as each new division of American troops reached the Front. But the situation was still precarious; the enemy was within forty miles of Paris and still threatened Amiens. It was imperative that the RAF keep vigilant for early signs of the Germans' next moves. The first day of June dawned fine and Belgrave in D5988 took to the air at 7.15am leading five other aircraft on a balloon-busting mission. He saw four kite balloons near Pys, between Bapaume and Albert, and attacked one of them from 6,000ft. His Lewis gun was armed with two rounds of Buckingham ammunition for every ordinary round. He emptied a drum at the balloon, starting from six hundred yards. Belgrave reported: 'The observer jumped out in a white parachute and I fired a burst at him, as he glided down, at close range. The balloon sank and later when I recrossed the lines I saw it deflated at the side of a track.' There are interesting points here. Despite scores of incendiary bullets hitting the balloon, it did not catch fire. Belgrave's words are also a reminder that balloon observers and some German fliers were issued with parachutes while, because of disgraceful bureaucratic intransigence, British pilots in the Great War never were. Finally, some may think it was at best unsporting to attempt to riddle an enemy with bullets as he dangled helplessly beneath his canopy but it is probably wise for anyone who has never been in action to refrain from comment. Immediately after downing the balloon Belgrave headed north, climbing to 8,000ft, and spotted a German two-seater near the village of Gomiécourt, not to be confused with Gommecourt, notorious hot spot in the opening stages of the Battle of the Somme. He tried to attack but failed to get close enough as the German dived east. Belgrave landed back at Boffles with only three other aircraft; Gordon Duncan had returned earlier after a stud on his engine sump plate popped out and Lewis had to make a forced landing at Bellevue in B151 with a failed oil pump. That evening Belgrave took D5988 on a roving commission but failed to find any enemy aircraft. Incidentally, he and later Art Duncan were among only a few pilots of the squadron granted permission to go on these freelance expeditions.

Next day Belgrave and Saunders again teamed up for a 4.30am start to patrolling, taking Lewis with them. After forty minutes in the air Belgrave spotted a two-seater north of Albert at 6,000ft. At first he thought it might be British as there was a lot of white in its markings but as he flew closer he identified it as German and attacked. He fired a series of bursts from about 200 yards and he and Saunders chased the aircraft down to 2,500ft. By then Belgrave had emptied his Lewis drum and got a stoppage in his Vickers. The British pair last saw the two-seater scurrying east at low altitude near La Boisille before it vanished in the mist. Meanwhile poor Lewis had become hopelessly lost in the poor visibility and had to make a forced landing, fortunately without injury to himself or B151. Belgrave was not in action on June 3 but Art Duncan scored his tenth victory that evening when he shot shown an LVG over Contalmaison. The following afternoon Belgrave, Saunders and Lewis went on patrol and chased an enemy two-seater which they found north-east of Albert. They were unable to get up to the German's level so broke off to turn their attention to three kite balloons at Mametz Wood. Belgrave, with D5988's Lewis gun partly loaded with Buckingham, fired on one of the balloons as he closed the range from five hundred yards down to two hundred yards' range and he reckoned up to fifty bullets struck home. Two of the balloons were hauled down, still inflated, and the observer bailed out of one.

The trio of Belgrave, Pat Saunders and Glyn Lewis was in action again on June 5, this time against opponents considerably more formidable than kite balloons. Gordon Duncan took off with them at 6pm but before any enemy was sighted he had to land at Bellevue when the engine of C9498 seized. It was 7.30pm when the remaining three SE5s found up to thirteen brightly-coloured Fokker triplanes of the type forever associated with the Red Baron. Officially designated Dr1, these single-seat machines were not particularly quick but had a great rate of climb and were light and sensitive and could turn on the proverbial sixpence. In skilled hands they were opponents to be reckoned with. As Belgrave approached the Germans at 15,000ft over Proyart, south-east of Albert, he counted six triplanes with a formation of another five or seven below them. Despite the unfavourable odds, he led his patrol into an attack. After a few minutes Sopwith Camels of No 201 Squadron arrived on the scene and there followed fully half an hour of intense, confused and exhausting fighting. It was a classic air battle with up to sixteen aircraft dodging, jinking and zooming with the ever-present risk of being shot down or colliding mid-air with friend or foe. The British machines dived to the attack time and again on the darting Fokkers, a flash of coloured wing or fuselage appearing in gun sights only to vanish as the German pilots threw their machines into evasive manoeuvres. Early in the scrap Belgrave dived D5988 at a green triplane and put two short bursts into it. 'The EA swung over and did two corkscrew turns, then dived and hit the ground and burst into flames,' Belgrave said in his combat report. Saunders, in B137, saw the doomed Fokker going down but was too busy battling with the German's comrades to watch it crash. Pilots of No 201 confirmed Belgrave's victory, his fifteenth. Belgrave finally had to break off and lead his patrol home because their fuel was running out. Three other squadron members had been balloon-bursting earlier in the day and succeeded in destroying one balloon each. Art Duncan sent down one of them in flames at Irles, the observer bailing out. It was to be Duncan's last victory with the squadron for he was posted to home establishment later in the month.

Next afternoon Belgrave, Saunders and Gordon Duncan went on an operational patrol but any hopes of further triplane-bashing went unfulfilled. Duncan had to turn home after an hour when the carburettor of B151 started playing up. Belgrave and Saunders stuck it out for two hours but, apart from seeing a lone German over Bapaume, they returned home with nothing to report. Belgrave was unable to find any enemy aircraft when he took D5988 on a roving commission on June 7. Perhaps through frustration he decided to see if could at least harry the Germans on the ground. He dropped to 1,000ft over the southern outskirts of Albert and, spotting a lone enemy soldier, dived on him and fired fifty rounds from four hundred to two hundred yards. As Belgrave zoomed away he lost sight of the man and was unable to tell whether he had been hit or simply dived for cover in a trench.

Apart from ten minutes of practice flying, Belgrave rested the following day but he and Saunders were back in action with decisive results on June 9. They took off with Glyn Lewis and Gordon Duncan at 9.30am. Duncan's B8398 suffered engine failure caused by faulty interrupter gear and he had to make a forced landing at Pas. The machine was a write-off and he suffered head injuries serious enough to put him in hospital and keep him away from the squadron for a month. Meanwhile Belgrave and Saunders had found their prey at 7,000ft north-east of Arras. Belgrave saw seven or eight Hannover CL two-seaters and when one of them became separated from the formation he put D5988 into a dive to get under its tail and gave it a burst from thirty feet away. Saunders, in B137, attacked from the side and fired his Vickers. The enemy machine turned several times and when Belgrave pulled out, Saunders got on the German's tail and gave him a close burst from both guns. The Hannover went into a vertical dive with Belgrave again on its tail. Enveloped in flames, it crashed near Boyelles. Five minutes later the British pair found six more Hannover two-seaters well over the German side of the lines at 10,000ft. Belgrave attacked the highest of the enemy aircraft but gun problems meant he could only fire about ten rounds. However, two bursts hit home at very close range and the German observer slumped over the side, dead or wounded. The engine also appeared to have been hit as the two-seater went down in a series of stall turns. Saunders, who had got in several longer bursts, followed the stricken German down but was also plagued with gun stoppages. Both British pilots pulled out to rectify the problems, caused by cross-feeds, and were unable to see whether the German crashed.

Belgrave had chalked up his sixteenth and seventeenth victories, both shared with Saunders. Unlucky Lewis crashed an hour and a half into the patrol while trying to land B151 at Bellevue. He was not injured and hard-worked B151 was repaired. With mid-summer approaching it was light enough for Belgrave and Saunders to be in the air again at 4am the following day for a two-hour patrol. They saw only one German in two hours and did not engage it. The two comrades who had shared so much success in aerial combat were not to know it but as they landed at 6am for breakfast they had flown together for the last time.

# CHAPTER SIX

# THY WILL BE DONE

THURSDAY June 13. Shortly before 4am Allied time – the Germans were an hour ahead at that period – James Belgrave studied the sky above the flatlands surrounding Boffles airfield to assess whether it was a good day to go hunting the Hun. It was cloudy and visibility would not be the best but the Captain was ready for action. He was reasonably well rested, having flown no patrols over the previous two days. His duties had consisted of brief flights to test aircraft and some paperwork to help out Major Moore. Somewhat bizarrely, the previous day Captain Scholte had presented Belgrave with a form requesting permission to apply for a patent. The inventive officer had dreamed up an idea for a multi-cylinder, two-stroke rotary engine for aircraft and had to sign an agreement effectively giving the Government rights over his brainchild. Belgrave duly signed to say he had given Scholte permission to go ahead with his patent request under those terms. Now in the cool dawn there were more pressing matters to be dealt with. Belgrave decided a patrol was possible and the three pilots he was to lead readied themselves. Belgrave was to fly his usual aircraft, D5988. He climbed into the cockpit and checked that the Vickers and Lewis were armed and serviceable, and that the fire extinguisher, Very pistol and his Colt automatic were safely stowed.

The most experienced of his pilots that day was Glyn Lewis, who had been in action with him several times. Lt Rhys Glyndore Lewis, a slightly built chap whose widowed mother lived in Merthyr Tydfil, had reached the RAF via the South Wales Borderers. His father had been an assistant manager in a steelworks. Lewis was in C9498. Lt Henry Gordon, who had joined the squadron only the previous month, was from Durham, Ontario. He was given E1261 for what was to be his first flight over German territory. John Macvicker was piloting the fourth SE5a of the flight, D6183. The 20-year-old lieutenant, whose father was a doctor and JP in Street, Somerset, was going up merely to see the lines. Perhaps because he had not had enough experience with the squadron, he would not be going over enemy territory. The patrol took off at 4.15am.

After half an hour Belgrave spotted a likely prey, an enemy two-seater of unidentified type, and dived on it from 9,000ft with Lewis and Gordon following. Gordon fired about forty rounds, starting at four hundred yards' range. Belgrave was still on the enemy aircraft's tail as they dived to about 3,000ft. With the German trying to shake off his determined pursuer, Gordon lost sight of both aircraft when they were swallowed by the ground mist about four miles east of Albert. Gordon turned to follow Lewis, who was heading south-east and losing height. They crossed the River Somme and, about twelve miles from the scene of the encounter with the German aircraft, Lewis landed with engine trouble between Ablaincourt and Chaulnes, smashing his undercarriage in the process. Gallantly, Gordon landed to see what he could do to help. Within a few moments German soldiers approached and started firing. Gordon immediately ran back to his aircraft, calling to Lewis to follow and climb aboard with him. Lewis either mistook the troops as friendly despite them firing or, realising they were Germans, decided to give Gordon the chance to get off. Whatever his reasoning, he walked towards the soldiers. Gordon reported: 'I called to him again and as the soldiers were still firing I took off. I circled back and dived over the body of men intending to fire but saw Lt Lewis in their midst so did not do so as I was afraid of hitting him.' Gordon got back to Boffles at 5.30am where he found that a longeron and one of the rudder control wires of his aircraft were practically shot away. Gordon was praised for such a creditable performance on his first patrol and was given joint credit for Belgrave's eighteenth victory after an anti-aircraft battery reported that the German aircraft had 'apparently crashed out of control'.

Macvicker landed safely at 6am but of Belgrave there was no sign. The squadron feared the worst, particularly after the battery confirmed that a British machine also went down in the fight they witnessed. Whether Belgrave became disoriented in the mist and crashed or was shot down, either from the ground or by the two-seater's gunner, is likely to remain a mystery. The German records are incomplete. Unteroffizier Joern and Leutnant R Clauditz in a two-seater were credited with one SE, their first victory, that day. Norman Macmillan, in notes for a proposed history of No 45 Squadron, stated that Belgrave was shot down and killed by Leutnant Lehmann, though unfortunately he quoted no source for the information. Wilhelm Lehmann, the 25-year-old commander of Jasta 5, then based at Villers-sur-Nicole, is credited in German records with downing an SE5a, his fourth and final victory, on June 13. However, the action took place over Bouzincourt, five or six miles from where Belgrave crashed, and Gordon made no mention of seeing a German single-seater in the vicinity. Lehmann himself was killed over Albert only thirteen days later.

At Boffles, uncertainty over the fate of an officer, even one as valued and well-liked as Belgrave, could not be allowed to disrupt squadron duties. Later in the morning of June 13 Scholte led a four-aircraft patrol which tackled a pair of Hannover two-seaters with inconclusive results. That afternoon there was formation flying practice for other pilots. Pat Saunders took temporary command of Belgrave's B Flight and continued his friend's good work with typical vigour. When he was sent home in August Saunders had scored twelve victories and been awarded the squadron's first Distinguished Flying Cross. The day after Belgrave failed to return Major Moore wrote to the missing pilot's parents. He would have been expected to praise their son, of course, but the tributes in Moore's letter went far beyond those dictated by good form in such circumstances. His words are worth giving in full:

> Your son's machine failed to return last evening from patrol. He was last seen by another member of the patrol fighting a Hun at 3,000ft. Both machines disappeared into the mist at 2,000ft and the anti-aircraft inform us that they saw the fight and think both machines went down. This does not necessarily mean your son was killed and his engine may have been hit and failed to pick up and forced him to land. I only hope this is the case.
>
> Your son has been commanding the squadron during my temporary absence. I can hardly tell you what an irreparable loss your son is to us. He has done magnificently and has

brought down ten Hun machines in barely six weeks. Not only that but he has raised the pilots to the highest pitch of enthusiasm and No 60 has not had a better flight commander. I am positive that had he remained with us your son would have won the highest awards.

He was literally loved by us all and the men adored him, referring to him as the Captain. As you know, he received a well-earned bar to his MC a short time ago and as a little incident of the men's appreciation of him the following shows *(sic)*. He had in his Flight a box in which he left his kit. A few days after he found it mysteriously painted and the MC appeared on it and when he got his bar they put the rose on the MC. As for the officers, he was their ideal and they admired him for the hero he was. As for myself, I knew your son at Rochford and I knew before he came to me what a splendid chap he was. I was delighted when I knew he was coming to me and his loss is irreplaceable. I have lost my best officer and I have lost a friend. I only pray he is safe on the other side. All my officers wish to express their heartfelt sympathy to you and I assure you never were sincerer words uttered. The lads would have followed your son anywhere, never had pilots more complete confidence in their leader. As for myself, my grief is beyond words and I trust your brave and gallant son will be spared to you. He is one of our great men both in prowess and in his personality.

Eventually a German aircraft dropped a message over the British lines confirming that Belgrave had been killed on June 13 and Lewis captured uninjured. The news prompted another pilot – again, it is not known which – to write to Belgrave's mother. The message, in heartfelt terms that a more cynical generation would shy from using, said: 'I cannot tell you how we worshipped him. He was to us an ideal flight commander, one who knew no fear, who had no favourites and who played the game with all the zest of a sportsman and Briton. He kept us full of enthusiasm and keenness and his almost daily successes filled us with the keen desire for emulation. He was as modest as he was brave, and as true as he was staunch. Personally I loved him and admired him, not only as a true friend but as a man. We are sorrowful but proud of "Jimmy". He gave his life to England but his soul to God.'

It is a sobering thought that of the members of Belgrave's last patrol only Lewis was to survive the war. Plucky Henry Gordon was killed on July 7. He was on his second patrol of the day and was with Macvicker and four other pilots of B Flight when they had a scrap with a Fokker. Gordon, in B137, was shot down near Villers-Bretonneux. Macvicker survived only until July 22. He was a member of an early-morning patrol that encountered a superior number of Pfalz aircraft over Aveluy Wood. One of the Germans was sent down out of control and another forced to land but at 5.40am Macvicker, in D6183, was shot down by Leutnant Emil Koch of Jasta 32. It was the fifth victory for the German, who increased his score to seven before being wounded by ground fire on a strafing mission in October. Before July was out fate robbed the squadron of another of Belgrave's most valued contemporaries, Captain Owen Scholte. When the telegram arrived at the home of Scholte's parents in West Heath, Hampstead, to notify them of their courageous son's death it was perhaps even harder for them to learn that he had been the victim of a simple motor accident. No 60 Squadron's new CO, Major Cyril Crowe, appointed when Major Moore was promoted and given a new posting, had taken advantage of poor flying weather to accept a dinner invitation from No 41 Squadron. On July 29 he took Scholte with him to the rendezvous in Dieppe where officers from several squadrons of 13th Wing were dining. Scholte was particularly pleased as former No 60 Squadron comrade Captain Frank Soden, now with No 41, was there. For the trip home after the party Crowe took the wheel of the Crossley tender himself as his driver was unwell. Soden and three other No 41 Squadron officers decided to accompany Crowe and Scholte part of the way. At 11.45pm Crowe crashed when he missed a sharp turn in the tree-lined road. In the mist a gap where two trees were missing had fooled him into thinking the road went straight on. Scholte was thrown against the trunk of a tree and was found lying in the middle of the road bleeding badly. He died in hospital with a fractured skull the following day. Major Cyril Foggin, aged 26, from Newcastle upon Tyne, died from similar injuries. Crowe was reprimanded by a court martial and reduced to Captain for a month but went on to command No 85 Squadron. He would not have been driving on the fateful night, or even commanding No 60 Squadron, had it not been for another tragic twist of chance.

Moore's job was to have gone to Major James McCudden, VC, DSO and Bar, MC and Bar, MM and Croix de Guerre. McCudden, with 57 victories to his credit, set off to fly to Boffles on July 9. Uncertain of his exact position because of the poor visibilty, he landed at Auxi-le-Chateau, where No 8 and No 52 Squadrons were based, to get his bearings. Learning he was less than five miles from his intended destination, he took off again but appeared to stall during a steep turn, perhaps as a result of his engine choking because of an incorrect carburettor being fitted. His SE5a dived into the ground and McCudden died that evening. It is particularly ironic if technical problems were to blame for the ace's death for McCudden had risen through the ranks from mechanic and was meticulous about aircraft preparation. No 60 Squadron ended the war at the former German airfield of Quievy, ten miles east of Cambrai. Alexander Beck, the pilot sent home temporarily for being too young, scored the squadron's last victory during a solo patrol on November 1.

In England, meanwhile, Dalrymple and Isabella Belgrave endured the torment of not knowing where their son was buried. He lay in German-held territory, of course, and the Commonwealth War Graves Commission has no record of precisely when his grave was found by the Allies as they advanced towards victory in the months leading to the Armistice of November 11. At some point James Belgrave was re-interred in Grove Town Cemetery at Méaulte, south of Albert and about three miles from where he fell. The cemetery was established on the site of a casualty clearing station set up in 1916 to deal with casualties from the Somme battlefields. The last burials are thought to have been in September 1918. However, as late as March 1921 the Air Ministry noted that Belgrave's grave had not yet been definitely located so it is not known when his parents learned of his final resting place. In the weeks immediately following James's death they were occupied dealing with formalities. The Belgraves produced an obituary for use in the local Press. The *Oxford Chronicle* and the *Bucks Free Press* ran the tribute in their columns on July 12. The *Oxford Times* followed suit next day and an edited-down version appeared in the *Bucks Herald* on July 27. There was also paperwork to be completed concerning James's estate of £837 as he had left no will. A reminder of their son's gallantry, though no reminder was needed, came three months after his death when the award of the Bar to his MC was listed in the *London Gazette*. According to squadron historian Joe Warne, by war's end the tally of awards won during service in No 60 amounted to one VC, two DSOs, three Bars to the DSO, twenty MCs and three

Bars and six DFCs. The cost: fifty-seven aircrew members killed in action and another fourteen killed in accidents or died of injuries. The Belgraves were also entitled to claim the 1915 Star, Victory Medal and British War Medal earned by James.

At the end of the year Bedford School wrote to the Belgraves seeking information about James's life to be included in a permanent record of the old boys who fell. There was also a request for a donation towards a memorial. It was perhaps an indication that Dalrymple was in poor health that his wife dealt with that and subsequent correspondence. Through all this the Belgraves could at least console themselves with the knowledge that their elder son had come through the conflict unscathed. Charles Belgrave, aged 24 in late 1918, had served with distinction in the Camel Corps. He was to be seconded for service with the Egyptian government in the Frontier Districts Administration, stationed in the Western Desert at the Siwa Oasis, where he would find himself the only white man.

Was there a sweetheart to grieve for James Belgrave? Had he met a local girl while convalescing in Chinnor after Loos perhaps? We do not know. There are no letters to indicate a romance. There is also no clue to what James intended doing after the war. Whatever vague hopes he nurtured, a hectic existence confronting death in the sky virtually every day perhaps did not encourage detailed planning. What seems certain is that he possessed the will and temperament to succeed wherever he applied himself. A glance at his brother's career demonstrates what the Belgraves were capable of. After his stint in the desert and two years in Tanganyika, where he combined shooting big game with his duties in the Colonial Service, the newly-married Charles Belgrave obtained the post of Adviser to the Shaikh of Bahrain in 1926. For the following 31 years he guided the destinies of Bahrain, watching it develop from an obscure little Arab island, depending on pearl-diving, into a modern, oil-rich state. Charles Belgrave, knighted in 1952, was a talented artist and painter as the illustrations in a book he wrote about his time at Siwa prove. He also wrote his autobiography and numerous articles about eastern matters. Of course there is no suggestion that James's subsequent career would have mirrored that of his brother. He may well have wished to remain in uniform in peacetime. Of 30,122 officers in the RAF at the end of the war more than 26,000 were demobilised by January 1920 but, as a professional officer, perhaps Belgrave would have been permitted to stay on in the vastly reduced service or return to the Ox & Bucks.

Some of his wartime contemporaries continued their military careers successfully. Willie Read, who quit as No 45 Squadron's CO to go back to the cavalry, soon returned to the RFC and later commanded No 216 Squadron. After a short post-war break he rejoined the unit and moved it to Egypt. He retired as a Wing Commander in 1932. Van Ryneveld, his successor as Belgrave's commanding officer, ended the war as a full Colonel aged 27. He became the founding father and driving force of the South African Air Force before retiring in 1949 as General Sir Pierre Van Ryneveld. A sandy-haired young captain with a reputation as something of a disciplinarian arrived at No 45 a couple of weeks after Belgrave's departure. He retired as Marshal of the Royal Air Force Sir Arthur Harris GCB, OBE, AFC, LL D – better known as Bomber Harris, chief of Bomber Command during the Second World War. Geoffrey Cock, who flew with Belgrave from Ste-Marie-Cappel, was repatriated in December 1918 after four months as a prisoner of war, remained in the RAF and retired as a Group Captain in 1943. Norman Macmillan, another of Belgrave's comrades at No 45, wrote about his experiences in the First World War and maintained his links with flying. He was a war correspondent with the rank of Wing Commander in the Second World War. Cecil Lewis, who was with Belgrave on home defence, later flew with the Chinese air force and served with the RAF in the Second World War as well as being a renowned author. His 1930s classic *Sagittarius Rising* has already been mentioned but he was still writing fifty years later and his book *Pathfinder* was published in 1986. Others built careers away from aviation. For example, No 60 Squadron's Art Duncan returned to Canada after the war and became a leading professional ice hockey player. He died in his native Ontario in 1975.

Not all stories were so happy. Glyn Lewis, a prisoner of war for five months after the drama of June 13, was repatriated in time for Christmas of 1918. He left the RAF in 1919 and returned to the South Wales Borderers. He was sent to India with the 2nd Battalion in November of that year. Four months later Lewis was in the military hospital at Deolali, north-east of Bombay. What ailment took him there is not recorded but patients included men whose nerves had succumbed to the influence of drink, heat or danger and their tics gave rise to the old Army expression 'doolally tap'. Lewis was discharged from hospital but apparently failed to rejoin his battalion as instructed and was arrested at Jhansi. At a general court martial he denied being absent without leave but was sentenced to be dismissed the service. He arrived back in Britain on August 22

1921 to learn that the sentence had been quashed because the colonel presiding at his court martial had acted outside his powers. Instead Lewis was severely reprimanded and lost seniority, a sufficiently sad fate for one who had given so much during the testing days of 1918.

After the war James Belgrave's parents moved to the Isle of Wight where Dalrymple's mother had previously lived. On May 2 1922 Dalrymple died at the couple's home in Sandown, aged 71. Isabella, who later moved to Dorset where there were Belgrave relatives, died on December 10 1933, aged 72. James's brother Sir Charles survived into contented retirement, dying in 1969 when he was 74. In his autobiography *Personal Column* he made only one mention of James and then not by name. Sir Charles related how he was visited in Bahrain by 'an Army chaplain of very unorthodox style who had been in the Royal Flying Corps with my brother'. The unnamed pastor, on asking a taxi driver to take him to Charles Belgrave's house, was assured he would soon be with the Mustashar, the local term for adviser by which Belgrave was known. A comical exchange ensued between the driver and the chaplain, who was convinced he was being diverted to the home of a mysterious Mr Shaw.

The 1920s saw efforts by towns, villages, workplaces and schools to provide fitting and permanent memorials to those who had fallen in the war. James Belgrave is among the old boys listed on the panels of the Memorial Hall at Bedford School. The hall was opened in 1926 by Prince Henry, third son of George V. The Prince, at 26 too young to have served in the war, arrived in his dashing 10th Royal Hussars uniform. It is safe to assume no one reminded him of the embarrassment of having been selected as a godson for the Kaiser in 1900. Belgrave's was one of 454 names embossed on the panels. Recent research has turned up another 25 names that should have been included, necessitating another panel, and it seems three names were included in error. Whatever the precise figure, it was heartbreaking for masters who had taught the fallen – young men 'who walked off the playing fields and into the lines', as Cecil Lewis put it. Eleven places below Belgrave's name appears that of C D Booker, another air ace. Major Charles Dawson Booker, seven months younger than Belgrave, joined the Royal Naval Air Service direct from Bedford in September 1915. He was a brilliant exponent of the Sopwith Triplane. He later flew Camels as CO of No 201 Squadron and had scored 29 victories when he was shot down and killed protecting an inexperienced pilot in August 1918. It is estimated a total of more than 2,300 old boys had served, earning an impressive number of decorations, including three VCs, one posthumous. Belgrave is included also on a roll of honour compiled for the Borough of Bedford. Inside St John's, Territet, his name is on a memorial panel along with that of his cousin Amyas Willis and other British men with local connections.

The name of James Belgrave is carved on the village war memorial in Chinnor and appears on a wooden panel in the church along with those of two other officers and thirty-three men who died. North Kilworth also claimed Belgrave as one of its own. He is among the nine Great War dead commemorated on the memorial on the village green. His uncle Colonel Dacres Belgrave played a leading part in the dedication ceremony in 1920. The names originally appeared on a tablet in rank order, with Belgrave's coming second to that of Brigadier General Kenna VC, hero of Omdurman killed by a sniper in Gallipoli. After the Second World War, when four more names had to be accommodated on the memorial, the names from the previous conflict were rearranged in alphabetical order with no mention of rank. Belgrave's name was still the second, but behind that of Victor Ball, a private soldier who died in the same month as him. Inside St Andrew's church, North Kilworth, Belgrave's name is listed on a memorial scroll. But the most impressive memorial is a large brass plaque in the chancel. It was commissioned by the family and features the Belgrave arms and badges of the Ox & Bucks and RAF. The dedication states that Belgrave was awarded the bar to his MC on May 20 1918 after a month with 'Squadron 61, RAF'. He was, of course, with No 60 Squadron at the time. The inscription continues: 'Between that date and the day of his death he gained many air victories.' In the churchyard is the grave of James Belgrave's cousin Viola. After the war which robbed her of her sweetheart she had a house built overlooking the church and lived there unmarried, dedicating herself to village activities until her death aged 92 in 1976. Her headstone, in a style similar to those on the British war graves of the Western Front, bears the words Called To Higher Service.

Today an effort of imagination is required when tracing the sites of James Belgrave's war. Nature and the human hand have done much in ninety years to eradicate the scars of battle. There is nothing to indicate precisely where Belgrave was gassed at Loos. Some of his Ox & Bucks comrades, including Pierce Newton-King, who have no known grave, are among the 20,000 soldiers named on the memorial walls of Dud Corner cemetery outside Loos. The cemetery stands on the site of a German redoubt overlooking the drab flatness of the 1915 battlefield. This place has a desolate feel, particularly on a winter's day, despite the traffic roaring by on the Lens-to-Béthune road. At Ste-Marie-Cappel, the TGV rail line slices across the former landing ground where the ghosts of No 45 Squadron's Strutters do nothing to hinder the trains on their dash to or from the Channel Tunnel. The uninitiated would never realise the RFC was there. Amid hop fields near Poperinghe, however, the headstones of Belgrave's No 45 Squadron comrades Greenhow, Lubbock, Bowden, Stevenson and Thompson stand in immaculate line in Lijssenthoek military cemetery and tell their own silent tale. As a footnote on Belgrave's friend and mentor Lubbock, it is worth mentioning that his nephew, the present Lord Avebury, was named after him. The peer is perhaps better known as Eric Lubbock MP, who took Orpington for the Liberals in 1962.

At Boffles, whatever traces No 60 Squadron left in 1918 have vanished from the farmland where the airfield stood. Henry Gordon, one of the two pilots who returned here from Belgrave's last patrol, is buried at Harbonnieres, between Amiens and St Quentin. The other, John Macvicker, lies in Gauchy-Cauchy cemetery, north of the Arras-Cambrai road.

James Belgrave's last resting place, Grove Town Cemetery, is near the aerospace complex at Méaulte yet has an isolated feel as it is set amid wide fields on a route more farm track than road. The cemetery, where 1,394 war dead are buried, was designed by Sir Edwin Lutyens, who was responsible for the Cenotaph in London and the massive Thiepval memorial that dominates the Somme battlefields. Perhaps because it was one of the last in the cemetery, Belgrave's grave is a little separated from the tight lines of other headstones and stands in a plot next to the plinth of the large memorial stone which bears the tribute Their Name Liveth For Evermore. Belgrave is buried alongside Gunner Tom Greenwood, from Burnley, Lancs, who died aged 24 on August 24 1918 while serving with the Royal Field Artillery. Carved upon James Belgrave's stone are a cross and the badge of the RAF. Beneath them are the words chosen by his family and repeated on the plaque in the church at North Kilworth.

Thy Will Be Done.

# BIBLIOGRAPHY

Barker, Ralph. *The Royal Flying Corps in France.* Constable 1994

Belgrave, C Dalrymple. *Siwa, the Oasis of Jupiter Ammon.* John Lane The Bodley Head 1923

Belgrave, Sir Charles. *Personal Column.* Hutchinson & Co 1960

Bowyer, Chaz, editor. *Royal Flying Corps Communiques 1917-1918.* Grub Street 1998

Cherry, Niall. *Most Unfavourable Ground. The Battle of Loos 1915.* Helion & Company 2005

Cole, Christopher, editor. *Royal Air Force Communiques 1918.* Tom Donovan Publishing 1990

Cole, Christopher, and E F Cheesman. *The Air Defence of Great Britain 1914-1918.* The Bodley Head 1984

De-la-Noy, Michael. *Bedford School. A History.* Bedford School 1999

Farnham, George F. *Leicestershire Medieval Village Notes Vol III*

Foster, Joseph. *The Descendants of John Backhouse, Yeoman.* Chiswick Press 1894

Franks, Norman, with Frank Bailey and Russell Guest. *Above The Lines.* Grub Street. 1993

Franks, Norman, with Russell Guest & Frank Bailey. *Bloody April...Black September.* Grub Street 1995

Franks, Norman, with Frank Bailey and Rick Duiven. *The Jasta War Chronology.* Grub Street. 1998

Franks, Norman, with Frank Bailey and Rick Duiven. *The Jasta Pilots.* Grub Street 1996

Franks, Norman. *Who Downed the Aces in WWI?* Grub Street. 1996

Gilbert, Martin. *First World War.* BCA 1994

Henshaw, Trevor. *The Sky Their Battlefield.* Grub Street 1995

Jefford, C G. *The Flying Camels.* Published by C G Jefford 1995

Lewis, Cecil. *Sagittarius Rising.* Peter Davies Ltd 1936

Macdonald, Lynn. *1915 The Death of Innocence.* Headline 1993

Macmillan, Norman. *Into the Blue.* Jarrolds 1969

Nichols, John. *History and Antiquities of Leicestershire Vol IV*

O'Byrne, William. *Naval Biographical Dictionary.* 1849

O'Connor, Mike. *Airfields & Airmen, Arras.* Pen & Sword Military 2004

O'Connor, Mike. *Airfields & Airmen, The Channel Coast.* Pen & Sword Military 2005

O'Connor, Mike. *Airfields & Airmen, Somme.* Leo Cooper. 2002

O'Connor, Mike. *Airfields & Airmen, Ypres.* Leo Cooper. 2001

Paget, Guy. *The History of the Althorp and Pytchley Hunt.* Collins 1937

Scott, A J L. *Sixty Squadron RAF 1916-1919.* William Heinemann 1920

Shores, Christopher, with Norman Franks & Russell Guest. *Above the Trenches.* Grub Street 1990

Steel, Nigel, and Peter Hart. *Tumult in The Clouds.* Hodder & Stoughton 1997

Swann, Major General J C. *The Citizen Soldiers of Buckinghamshire 1795-1926.* Hazell Watson & Viney 1930

Warner, Philip. *The Battle of Loos.* William Kimber 1976

*Backhouse & Company.* A Barclays Publication

*Chronicle of the Oxfordshire & Buckinghamshire Light Infantry.* Eyre & Spottiswode 1916

*A History of Banks, Bankers and Banking in Northumberland, Durham and Yorkshire.* Maberly Phillips

*Shotley Bridge. A Village Survey and Brief History.* Shotley Bridge Village Community Trust 1989

*Victoria County History. Leicestershire Volume*

*Cross & Cockade,* various issues

# INDEX